# Business Education

**Lee Coutts** and **Alistair Wylie**

# Acknowledgements

The Publishers would like to thank the following for permission to reproduce copyright material:

**Photo credits**

Page 3 © FirstGroup plc; page 4 (top) © FirstGroup plc, (bottom) © Unite; page 5 © Andrey Prokhorov/iStockphoto; page 6 (top) © Paul Brown/Rex Features, (bottom) © Peter Lawson/Rex Features; page 7 © Chris McNulty/Alamy; page 8 (top) © FirstGroup plc, (bottom) © Paul Brown/Rex Features; page 11 (top) © Greenpeace, (bottom) © Steve Morgan/Greenpeace; page 12 (both) © BP p.l.c.; page 15 © ANDREW MILLIGAN/PA Archive/Press Association Images; page 16 © Alex Segre/Rex Features; page 21 © Monkey Business/Fotolia.com; page 22 (top) © Shane Shaw/iStockphoto, (bottom) © Forsyth Glazing Ltd (www.forsythglazing.co.uk); page 23 (top) © David Burner/Rex Features, (centre) © Oliver Rudkin/UCF/Rex Features, (bottom) © Oxfam; page 25 © Stockbyte/Photolibrary Group Ltd; page 27 (from top) © Yuri Arcurs – Fotolia, © moodboard/Corbis, © Sean Locke/istockphoto.com, © TravelStockCollection – Homer Sykes/Alamy, © The Royal Bank of Scotland, © ANDREW MILLIGAN/PA Archive/Press Association Images; page 28 (from top) © Yuri Arcurs – Fotolia, © Monkey Business – Fotolia, © NEWS PICTURES/Rex Features; page 29 (left from top) Used with permission from McDonald's Corporation, © Steve Meddle/Rex Features, © Royal Mail plc, © Oxfam, (right from top) © Virgin Holidays, © Google, © Thomson Holidays, © Red Cross; page 32 © nyul – Fotolia; page 33 (top) © michaeljung/Fotolia.com, (bottom) © Uyen Le/©iStockphoto.com; page 34 (from top) ©Photodisc/Getty Images, © Comstock Images/Photolibrary Group Ltd, © Design Pics Inc/Rex Features; page 39 © European Union; page 40 (top) © The Prince's Trust, (bottom) © Business Gateway /Crown Copyright; page 41 (from top) © Royal Mail plc, © Steve Meddle/Rex Features, © Oxfam, © Google; page 43 © The Royal Bank of Scotland Group. ™ is/are trade marks of the RBS Group.; page 44 (from top) © kristian sekulic/iStockphoto.com, © oliver leedham/Alamy, © Image Source/Corbis; page 46 (top) © Russell Binns/Alamy, (bottom) © Prisma Bildagentur AG/Alamy; page 47 © Evgeny Tyzhinov – Fotolia.com; page 52 © John Molloy/Digital Vision/Getty Images; page 53 (top) © H. Mark Weidman Photography/Alamy, (bottom) © Kirsty Pargeter/Fotolia.com; page 54 (top) © Aleksandar Radovanov, (bottom) © iQoncept/Fotolia.com; page 55 © Radovan Marček/Fotolia.com; page 58 © Yuri Arcurs/Fotolia.com; page 59 (top) © Sean Gladwell – Fotolia.com, (bottom) ©Photodisc/Getty Images; page 60 (from top) © iStockphoto.com/sweetym, © Jacob Wackerhausen/iStockphoto, © STEVE LINDRIDGE/Alamy; page 61 (from top) © AshDesign/Fotolia.com, © Pavel Losevsky – Fotolia, © Hodder Education, © Andrey Prokhorov/iStockphoto; page 62 (both) © Tim Scrivener/Rex Features; page 63 © William Tracey Group; page 64 © Dariusz Kopestynski – Fotolia; page 65 © Gareth Leung – fotolia.com; page 66 © Andrey Prokhorov/iStockphoto; page 67 (top) © Yuri Arcurs/Fotolia.com, (bottom) ©Martin Firus/istockphoto.com; page 68 (from top) © Alexey – Fotolia, © slobo/iStockphoto, ©Uyen Le/iStockphoto.com, © Dmitriy Chistoprudov – Fotolia.com; page 70 (top) © deanm1974 – Fotolia, (bottom left) © Helen King/CORBIS, (bottom right) © Photomac/Fotolia.com.

Every effort has been made to trace all copyright holders, but if any have been inadvertently overlooked the Publishers will be pleased to make the necessary arrangements at the first opportunity.

Although every effort has been made to ensure that website addresses are correct at time of going to press, Hodder Gibson cannot be held responsible for the content of any website mentioned in this book. It is sometimes possible to find a relocated web page by typing in the address of the home page for a website in the URL window of your browser.

Hachette UK's policy is to use papers that are natural, renewable and recyclable products and made from wood grown in sustainable forests. The logging and manufacturing processes are expected to conform to the environmental regulations of the country of origin.

Orders: please contact Bookpoint Ltd, 130 Milton Park, Abingdon, Oxon OX14 4SB. Telephone: (44) 01235 827720.
Fax: (44) 01235 400454. Lines are open 9.00–5.00, Monday to Saturday, with a 24-hour message answering service.
Visit our website at www.hoddereducation.co.uk. Hodder Gibson can be contacted direct on:
Tel: 0141 848 1609; Fax: 0141 889 6315; email: hoddergibson@hodder.co.uk

© Lee Coutts and Alistair Wylie 2011
First published in 2011 by
Hodder Gibson, an imprint of Hodder Education,
An Hachette UK Company
2a Christie Street
Paisley PA1 1NB

Impression number     5 4 3 2 1
Year                  2014 2013 2012 2011

All rights reserved. Apart from any use permitted under UK copyright law, no part of this publication may be reproduced or transmitted in any form or by any means, electronic or mechanical, including photocopying and recording, or held within any information storage and retrieval system, without permission in writing from the publisher or under licence from the Copyright Licensing Agency Limited. Further details of such licences (for reprographic reproduction) may be obtained from the Copyright Licensing Agency Limited, Saffron House, 6–10 Kirby Street, London EC1N 8TS.

Cover photo © Dmitriy Shironosov/iStockphoto
Illustrations by Emma Golley at Redmoor Design and Tech-Set Ltd, Gateshead
Typeset in 10/13.5 Myriad Light by Tech-Set Ltd, Gateshead
Printed in Italy

A catalogue record for this title is available from the British Library
ISBN: 978 1444 122718

# Contents

**Introduction** .................................................... v

## Part 1

**Social Studies Outcomes:**
People in society, economy and business

1. SOC 4–19a ............................................. 2
2. SOC 4–19b ............................................. 10
3. SOC 4–20a ............................................. 14
4. SOC 4–20b ............................................. 20
5. SOC 4–20c ............................................. 32
6. SOC 4–21a ............................................. 37
7. SOC 4–21b ............................................. 43
8. SOC 4–22a ............................................. 50
9. SOC 4–22b ............................................. 58

**Technologies Outcomes:**
Business contexts for developing technological skills and knowledge

10. TCH 4–01c, TCH 4–05a, TCH 4–06a, TCH 4–07a, TCH 4–07b ... 64

## Part 2

**Value Added Tasks (VATs)**

VAT 1 ..................................................... 74
VAT 2 ..................................................... 76
VAT 3 ..................................................... 78
VAT 4 ..................................................... 79
VAT 5 ..................................................... 81
VAT 6 ..................................................... 82
VAT 7 ..................................................... 83
VAT 8 ..................................................... 85
VAT 9 ..................................................... 87

**Appendices** ............................................. 92

**Mapping grid** .......................................... 94

**Index** ..................................................... 96

# Introduction

**Welcome to Curriculum for Excellence (CfE) for Business Education level 4.** This book has been written to support the new experiences and outcomes of Curriculum for Excellence. In particular, it focuses on the level 4 outcomes relating to Business Education. These are mainly to be found as part of the Social Studies experiences and outcomes and Technologies experiences and outcomes. Opportunities for the development of outcomes in Literacy and Numeracy have also been included where appropriate.

This book assumes that learners have completed the relevant Social Studies and Technologies experiences and outcomes at level 3.

## How to use this book

This book is arranged in two parts. Part 1 covers the relevant experiences and outcomes at level 4. Included within this are notes, activities and tasks. Reference is also made to other subject areas. The sections in Part 1 are arranged by order of outcome. These are mainly taken from the Social Studies outcomes although there is also reference to some of the Technologies outcomes. Whilst there is a connection to Business, the Technologies outcomes are more closely related to the existing subject area of Administration.

The authors have arranged Part 1 of the book as a development of their thoughts on how the experiences and outcomes *could* be approached and delivered. It is very much a starting point for further learning, teaching and development and should not be viewed as a definitive source or a textbook to be used as a template for a course. This would not support the ethos of Curriculum for Excellence.

Furthermore, Part 1 is laid out in order of the experiences and outcomes as defined in official documentation. This means that some themes and concepts are not tackled in a logical order if the experiences and outcomes were to be followed in numerical sequence.

Part 2 of the book contains a series of Value Added Tasks (VATs). These are designed to draw on the content of Part 1 of the book and to enable learners to integrate a variety of experiences and outcomes in a contextualised manner. Some tasks involve group work while others are for individual completion. There are also opportunities for self and peer assessment. All tasks have links to Literacy and/or Numeracy outcomes.

It is envisaged that teachers will adapt, develop and change these tasks to suit their own needs and those of their learners. Again, these tasks should not be seen as definitive in nature or content.

## About the authors

**Lee Coutts** and **Alistair Wylie** are experienced authors and educators in Business Education. Both have taught in the secondary and further education sectors and have experience of working in the national education arena. They have both published a wide variety of texts individually. This text is their first joint publication.

## Dedications

This book is dedicated to the memory of a dear friend, sadly missed.
Carol Millar: 28 February 1958 – 17 September 2010.


For Katie Coutts, one of the CfE pioneers.

# Part 1

**Social Studies Outcomes:**
People in society, economy and business

**Technologies Outcomes:**
Business contexts for developing technological skills and knowledge

# SOC 4–19a

## Definition of outcome | SOC 4–19a

I can present an informed view on how the expansion of power and influence of countries or organisations may impact on the cultures, attitudes and experiences of those involved.

## Introduction to outcome

In this outcome, we will focus on the expansion of power and influence of **organisations** and their impact. We will consider how the expansion and growth of two different companies has impacted on **cultures** and **attitudes** and the experience of those involved. This includes the impact on people affected by the organisations as well as those who run them.

### What this means

**Organisation** people who come together to achieve a common goal.

**Culture** the way that things are done.

**Attitude** different views and opinions.

We are going to use the following two organisations as we work through this outcome:

- **FirstGroup plc** (www.firstgroup.com)
- **Ryanair** (www.ryanair.com)

### Activity

It would be a good idea for you to visit each of their websites to find out information about each organisation. You may also use search engines to source additional information. If possible, you should spend some time doing this now and prepare a short report of your findings.

After working through this outcome you will be able to:

- understand the influence that organisations can have on culture
- understand the influence that organisations can have on people
- understand how organisations can impact on attitudes
- understand how organisations can expand
- describe the influence that organisations can have on culture
- describe the influence that organisations can have on people
- describe how organisations can impact on attitudes and practice
- describe how organisations can expand
- use examples from modern business to show the above.

# Development of outcome

Below are summaries of the main points relating to both FirstGroup plc and Ryanair. You should read this information and compare it to your findings from the activity on page 2.

## FirstGroup plc

FirstGroup plc was formed in 1989 and has its head office in Aberdeen, Scotland. Its main business is bus and rail transport. In the UK, it operates the largest bus network, with a fleet of some 8500 buses. Its rail operation is the largest in the UK, operating four **franchises** and one open access operator covering a quarter of the entire UK rail network. FirstGroup plc is currently the largest public transport provider in the UK.

FirstGroup plc is a public limited company but it was originally a publicly funded organisation.

### What this means

**Franchise**
a franchise gives someone the right to sell an established company's goods or services in a specific location using their name and logo, e.g. McDonalds.

### Activity

1. Describe possible business objectives for a public limited company.
2. Describe possible business objectives for a publicly funded organisation.
3. Explain reasons for the business objectives of FirstGroup plc changing following its conversion to a public limited company in 1995.

SOC 4-19a

One of FirstGroup plc's main objectives since becoming a public limited company has been to grow its main business areas and look for opportunities to develop new areas of business. Growth is mostly dependent on increasing passenger numbers but this is affected by several different factors:

- Punctuality and reliability – ensuring that public transport runs according to timetables.
- Safety – buses and trains are among the safest modes of transport. Ensuring that continues is key for public transport operators like FirstGroup to increase passenger numbers.
- Public transport is much more environmentally friendly than the private car. More customers are using public transport to reduce their own carbon footprint.
- External factors such as the recession and rising fuel costs can affect the numbers of passengers using public transport.

A FirstGroup train

FirstGroup plc has invested money to improve UK rail travel and has also developed new and innovative schemes for bus travel. It has also made safety its top priority. In order to achieve its objective of growth, FirstGroup plc moved into the American market in 1999. At first, it did this by buying small companies operating school buses. Over a period of several years, it has managed to build this up to around five per cent of all school bus contracts in the USA. It also bought businesses in Canada. FirstGroup plc has therefore had a significant impact on the transport industry in the UK, the USA and Canada.

### What this means

**UNITE union**
This is an organisation which represents the rights of workers. UNITE was formed when two other unions merged – the Transport and General Workers Union (TGWU) and AMICUS.

FirstGroup plc has also worked hard to attract and retain good staff. It has a partnership with the **UNITE union** in the UK to offer a network of learning centres for staff. These are designed to motivate staff by offering them the opportunity to undertake flexible learning in a variety of subjects including English, maths, computing skills and languages.

## What this means

**Corporate social responsibility**
this is about how companies manage their business so that it has an overall positive impact on society.

FirstGroup plc takes seriously its **corporate social responsibility** role believing that it has an opportunity to improve the environment. Increases in the number of people using public transport can help reduce traffic congestion and environmental pollution. Most recently, it has built a new 'green' corporate global headquarters.

## Revision tasks

1. State FirstGroup plc's main business objective since becoming a public limited company.
2. Describe the term 'franchise' (in your own words).
3. Explain how FirstGroup plc grew.
4. List the benefits of increased public transport.
5. Identify some positive aspects of the growth of FirstGroup plc in relation to people's attitudes towards public transport.
6. Identify some negative aspects of the growth of FirstGroup plc in relation to people's attitudes towards public transport.
7. Explain how a large transport company such as FirstGroup plc could ensure that it portrays a socially and environmentally responsible image to the public.

## Ryanair

Ryanair markets itself as a low fares airline. It started in business in 1985 in the Republic of Ireland. It has grown exponentially over the past 25 years to become one of the world's largest airlines employing over 8000 staff and carrying over 70 million passengers per year.

### What this means

**Restructure** rearranging the organisation of the business to make it more efficient.

**Stock Exchange** where you can buy and sell shares.

Ryanair was started by the Ryan family in 1985 with just one aircraft and one route. Despite its small beginnings, by the end of 1986 it had grown to carry 82,000 passengers and employ 151 staff. During the late 1980s, it continued to grow and acquire more aircraft and employ more staff. However, by 1990 it had accumulated losses totalling £20 million and was forced to **restructure** and change the way it worked. The Ryan family invested £20 million in the company and copied the business model of another airline to try to become the number one low-fares airline.

1991 was a difficult year in aviation as the Gulf War started and people were frightened to travel. This had a negative impact on staffing and passenger numbers. By 1992, Ryanair was still restructuring and cutting back its routes and fleet of aircraft. However, in 1993 the airline launched its first new route and, for the first time, passenger numbers were more than 1 million. Up to the end of 1996, increases in the number of routes offered and the purchase of more aircraft resulted in passenger numbers almost reaching 3 million.

1997 was a big year in the development of the company as it was floated on the **Stock Exchange** and became a public limited company. This was the year it also launched its third UK airport base at Glasgow Prestwick Airport, the first Ryanair base in Scotland.

In 2000, Ryanair launched its online booking website which quickly started taking over 50,000 bookings per week. By 2002, passenger numbers had climbed to over 10 million per year.

Ryanair's base at Prestwick Airport

Up until 2003, Ryanair had grown through investment and huge increases in passenger numbers year on year. This changed in 2003 when it acquired Buzz, a loss-making airline previously owned by KLM Royal Dutch Airlines.

In 2004, Ryanair was named the most popular airline on the Internet by Google and its website continued to be the most searched-for travel website in Europe. In 2005, passenger numbers were over 30 million as the airline continued to open up new airport bases across Europe. Since then and until the time of writing in 2010, Ryanair has continued to expand by opening new airport bases, buying new planes and increasing its staff and passenger numbers.

The growth and development of Ryanair over the past 25 years has had a significant impact on the use of air travel. In particular, it has made air travel more accessible to more people through the provision of low fares.

(Source: www.ryanair.com)

## Revision tasks

1. Describe the ways in which Ryanair has grown over the past 25 years.

2. Investigate and report on the impact that Ryanair's presence in different countries might have had on the local economy and employment. *Tip: You might want to use the Internet to search for information or news stories to help.*

3. Ryanair's actions have often caused controversy which has been reported in the news. Research one of these stories and summarise your findings. State the reasons why you think the company acted in the way it did.

4. 'Air travel and associated business cause major environmental damage.' Research this statement and produce a report to either support or disagree with this claim. Find out what steps airlines, such as Ryanair, are taking to offset their carbon emissions and how they are making their passengers more aware of this issue.

5. Explain how the attitude of the Chief Executive of Ryanair towards air travel might differ from that of one of the airline's passengers.

6. Complete the tables on the following page with examples relating to FirstGroup plc and Ryanair. You should identify the impact based on the action taken by the organisation. The first row in each table has been completed for you.

SOC 4-19a

## FirstGroup plc

| Action by organisation | Example of impact |
|---|---|
| Expansion into new markets. | More choice for consumers. |
| Takeover of existing businesses. | |
| Corporate social responsibility actions to reduce environmental impact. | |
| Change attitudes to the use of public transport by offering a better service. | |

## Ryanair

| Action by organisation | Example of impact |
|---|---|
| Provision of low fares. | Ability of consumers to travel to other countries. |
| Takeover of existing airline. | |
| Purchase of new, more fuel-efficient aircraft. | |
| Change to become a public limited company. | |

### Web links

You may find it useful to visit the following websites for more information about business organisations:

- www.businesslink.gov.uk
- www.carbontrust.co.uk

### Links to other subjects

This outcome links into several other subjects where you will have opportunities to further develop your skills, such as Geography and Literacy.

Business at National 4 and Business Management at National 5 give further consideration to business activities.

If you choose to study Environmental Science at National 4 or National 5, you may also have opportunities to learn more about the environment and the impact of business activity.

## What this means

**Attitude**  different views and opinions.

**Corporate social responsibility**  this is about how companies manage their business so that it has an overall positive impact on society.

**Culture**  the way that things are done.

**Franchise**  a franchise gives someone the right to sell an established company's goods or services in a specific location using their name and logo, e.g. McDonalds.

**Organisation**  people who come together to achieve a common goal.

**Restructure**  rearranging the organisation of the business to make it more efficient.

**Stock Exchange**  where you can buy and sell shares.

**UNITE union**  this is an organisation which represents the rights of workers. UNITE was formed when two other unions merged – the Transport and General Workers Union (TGWU) and AMICUS.

# SOC 4–19b

### Definition of outcome — SOC 4–19b

By examining the role and actions of selected international organisations, I can evaluate how effective they are in meeting their aims.

## Introduction to outcome

This outcome is focused on international business organisations. These are organisations which operate in more than one country.

We will consider the role of two different international organisations paying particular attention to their aims. We will also look at their actions in business and the world to evaluate how effective they are in meeting their aims.

After working through this outcome you will be able to:

- describe an international business organisation
- give examples of international business organisations
- give examples of the aims of different international business organisations
- describe the different roles that international business organisations can play
- describe how international business organisations operate
- evaluate how effective international business organisations are in meeting their aims.

## Development of outcome

This outcome will involve us researching different international organisations. We will use two different types of organisation to do this:

- Greenpeace
- British Petroleum (BP)

**This outcome is linked to outcome SOC 4–20b where we research the purposes and features of different types of organisations.**

## Greenpeace

Greenpeace is an independent global organisation that takes action to defend the natural world and promote peace. It exists to investigate, expose and confront environmental abuse by governments and corporations and to champion environmentally and socially responsible solutions, including scientific and technical innovation. It relies entirely on donations and does not accept funding from governments, corporations or political parties.

The Greenpeace ship 'Arctic Sunrise'

You may have seen it on the news or read about it online.

Greenpeace is frequently in the news because it takes nonviolent direct action around the world. Through its campaigning, it has been responsible for successfully stopping governments and large organisations from carrying out activities that cause damage to the environment.

### Activity

1. Visit the Greenpeace website (www.greenpeace.org.uk) to find out more about the organisation and its recent achievements.

2. Use the Internet to research the work of Greenpeace and its recent activity as reported in the news. Produce a short report of 300 words maximum.

## BP

BP is one of the world's largest energy companies, providing its customers with fuel for transportation, energy for heat and light, retail services and petrochemicals products for everyday items.

### Facts and figures

| | |
|---|---|
| **Sales and other operating revenues** | $239 billion (year 2009) |
| **Replacement cost profit** | $14.0 billion (year 2009) |
| **Number of employees** | 80,300 (at 31 Dec 2009) |
| **Proved reserves** | 18.3 billion barrels of oil equivalent |
| **Service stations** | 22,400 |
| **Exploration and production** | Active in 30 countries |
| **Refineries (wholly or partly owned)** | 16 |
| **Refining throughput** | 2.3 million barrels per day (year 2009) |

BP petrol station

BP tries to work in ways that will benefit the communities and habitats where it does business – and earn the world's respect. In other words, BP has a long-term commitment to the communities it works within. As such, it recognises a responsibility to create more than quick revenues from its investments. BP always strives to preserve and improve the surrounding environment, supporting enterprising businesspeople and encouraging energy-related education.

This is why, for example, it planned the construction schedule for the BTC pipeline (from the Caspian Sea to the Meditteranean coast) around the breeding season of a rare local grouse. And why it funded satellite transmitters to help experts track endangered sea turtles in the nearby seas.

It's why it has started programmes to share its business knowledge with entrepreneurs in Angola, South Africa, Trinidad and Tobago and elsewhere.

(Source: www.bp.com)

### Activity

1. Visit the BP website (www.bp.com) to find out more about the organisation and its recent achievements.

2. Use the Internet to research the work of BP and its recent activity as reported in the news. Produce a short report of 300 words maximum.

## Revision tasks

1. List what you believe to be the main aims of Greenpeace and BP.
2. How successful have Greenpeace and BP been in meeting these aims?
3. How do the activities of the two organisations differ from each other?
4. List areas of potential conflict between the two organisations.
5. List three stakeholders of each of the two organisations.

### Web links

- www.greenpeace.org.uk
- www.bp.com

### Links to other subjects

This outcome links into several other subjects where you will have opportunities to further develop your skills, such as Geography and Literacy.

Business at National 4 and Business Management at National 5 give further consideration to business activities and organisations.

If you choose to study Environmental Science at National 4 or National 5, you may also have opportunities to learn more about the environment and the impact of business activity.

# SOC 4–20a

## Definition of outcome — SOC 4–20a

I can examine critically how some economic factors can influence individuals, businesses or communities.

## Introduction to outcome

This outcome introduces the subject area of **economics** and the **basic economic problem**. It explores some of the reasons why **demand** for products in the economy change and consequentially, why some businesses fail.

### What this means

**Basic economic problem** resources to produce goods and services are limited and because we have unlimited desires for goods and services we are required to make a choice.

**Demand** the amount of people who wish to buy a product at a certain price and have the money to do so.

### What this means

**Recession** demand for goods and services is low and unemployment is high over a period of time.

After working through this outcome you will be able to:

- describe the term economics
- explain what is meant by the basic economic problem
- explain some of the reasons why businesses fail (in particular increased competition, changing demand and **recession**)
- explain the consequences of economic factors on the economy, business and individuals.

## Development of outcome

### The basic economic problem

You have probably heard the word 'economics' before; we hear it on the news, see it in newspapers and hear people talking about it. But what does it actually mean? Economics is about how the business world works and how it reacts to things that

are going on around it (sometimes known as the economic or external environment). It looks at how we make decisions regarding what goods and services to produce. Something that happens in one part of the world can have a huge impact upon another part. Decisions that are made by, for example, the Scottish Government can have an impact upon how businesses work in Scotland. This outcome aims to explore some of these.

Decisions have to be made by individuals, businesses and the government because of one main reason: there isn't enough money or goods/services in the world to be able to have everything that we want. As much as we might want everything (for example, nice clothes, a big house, lots of holidays) resources are limited so we can't have everything. **This is known as the basic economic problem.** Because of this, we have to make a choice, for instance, do we use our pocket money to buy a CD or do we buy a computer game? This is a decision that has to be made!

## Economic factors

Many new and existing businesses fail; in other words, they do not have the necessary resources (e.g. money) to continue to exist. Sometimes this is because of economic or external factors such as the ones shown in the diagram below.

Reasons why businesses sometimes fail

We need to explore some of the **economic factors** in depth.

(Poor management and other external factors are dealt with elsewhere in this book.)

## Too much competition

Businesses all face competition; it could be that a small butcher in your local high street has to compete against a larger retailer in the same town or one large retailer is having to compete against another one. In order to attract and keep customers, businesses have to offer incentives to customers to shop with them. These incentives could be special offers, lower prices or discounts. Because larger businesses have more power they can usually afford to have better incentives than smaller businesses and this can put smaller businesses out of business! Larger businesses can take advantage of **economies of scale** (discounts on bulk buying) and offer products cheaper than smaller retailers.

When new businesses open there are advantages:

- More choice of where to shop.
- Often cheaper products because of economies of scale.
- More jobs for people in the local community.
- The government gets more money from taxes.
- Better facilities (e.g. new roads).

However, when a business fails there are disadvantages:

- People are made **unemployed** (and there are large consequences of this).
- The government receives less money in tax and has to pay benefits to the unemployed.

### What this means

**Economies of scale** the benefits a business obtains from being large, e.g. discounts on bulk buying items.

## Not enough demand

Demand refers to how much people want something. When demand for a product is high (such as when a new product is launched) prices tend to be very high. This is because businesses can charge more money for the product that is in limited **supply**. As demand begins to decrease, businesses often decrease the price of the product in order to create more demand. This is why businesses have sales; the price of the product is reduced which encourages people to buy it (demand has increased).

Shops have sales to encourage people to buy their products

### What this means

**Unemployed** what a person who has no job is called.

**Supply** the amount of a product a supplier (manufacturer) is willing to produce at a certain price.

For example, Glasgow is well known for building ships on the River Clyde and the ships built there are now all over the world. However, because ships can be built more cheaply elsewhere in the world, demand for ships to be built in Glasgow has decreased. This has had many consequences for Glasgow.

## Recession

The United Kingdom up until early 2010 was said to be in a recession but what does this mean? When demand for goods and services is low and unemployment is high over a period of time, an economy is said to be in **recession.**

During a recession, many businesses fail and the number of people becoming unemployed increases. The consequences of this are a bit like a 'vicious circle' and can be shown in the following diagram:

The cycle of a recession

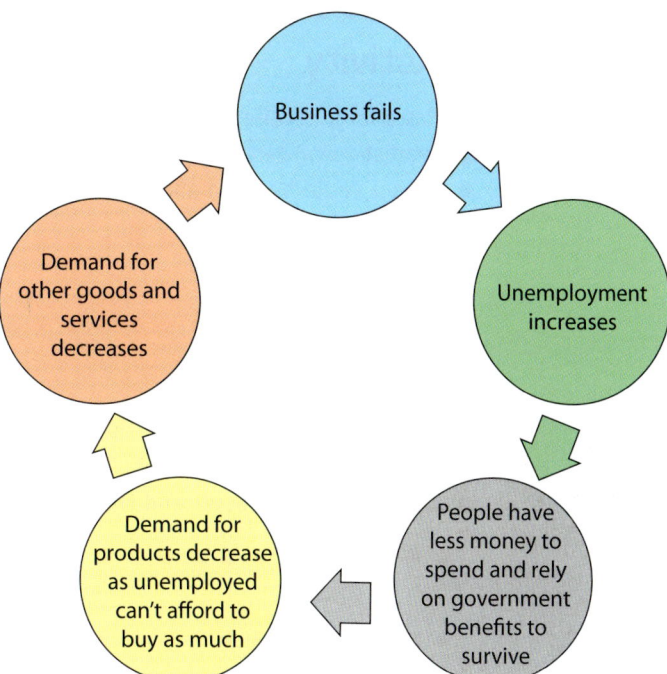

To help the economy come out of recession, the government will usually take action. This might include cutting interest rates, injecting money into specific parts of the economy and reducing VAT (Value Added Tax).

## Summary

We all live in an economy that is constantly changing. It is important to know what is happening around us because it will impact upon our lives and the lives of others. Businesses can fail because of different economic factors and this can have many consequences for us and the economy.

## Revision tasks

1. Describe what is meant by the term 'economics'.
2. Identify three reasons why businesses fail.
3. Identify three advantages of increased competition.
4. Explain what happens when a business decreases the price of its product.
5. What is a recession?
6. Outline the consequences of a recession.

### Activity

Has a large retailer (e.g. Tesco or ASDA) opened up in your town (or nearest town) recently? What impact has this had – remember the impact could be good and bad!

### Activity

In small groups, come up with as many consequences as you can of increasing unemployment. Think about the consequences for individuals, businesses and the local community.

### Activity

The United Kingdom was in recession during 2009 and the early part of 2010. Use the Internet to prepare a poster that outlines the actions the government took to help the country recover from recession.

## Links to other subjects

You will learn more about the structure of the UK and Scottish Governments in Modern Studies and/or Politics. You could also consider taking Economics as a subject at National 5 or Higher to explore economic issues in more detail.

### What this means

**Basic economic problem** resources to produce goods and services are limited and because we have unlimited desires for goods and services we are required to make a choice.

**Demand** the amount of people who wish to buy a product at a certain price and have the money to do so.

**Economies of scale** the benefits a business obtains from being large, e.g. discounts on bulk buying items.

**Recession** demand for goods and services is low and unemployment is high over a period of time.

**Supply** the amount of a product a supplier (manufacturer) is willing to produce at a certain price.

**Unemployed** if you have no job you are unemployed.

# SOC 4–20b

## Definition of outcome — SOC 4–20b

I can research the purposes and features of private, public and voluntary sector organisations to contribute to a discussion on their relationships with stakeholders.

## Introduction to outcome

This outcome is focused on different types of business organisations. Organisations are fundamental to the operation and success of business and may be public, private or voluntary in nature. We will consider the purpose and features of each type of business organisation.

Stakeholders are an important feature of every organisation and they have an important role to play. We will consider the importance and influence that stakeholders can have over different business organisations.

After working through this outcome you will be able to:

- describe the features of different types of business organisations:
    - private
    - public
    - voluntary
- describe the purpose of different types of business organisations:
    - private
    - public
    - voluntary
- research the features and purpose of different types of business organisations known to you in the business world
- describe different types of stakeholders
- describe the relationships that can exist between stakeholders and the interest they have in an organisation
- describe the influence that stakeholders can have over different business organisations.

(There are lots of new business terms in this outcome. At the end of this outcome you will find a 'What this means' section to help you understand these new words.)

## Development of outcome

Business organisations are part of our everyday lives. We interact with them, depend on them and work for them. In the world of business, we categorise them as belonging to one of three sectors of business:

- Private
- Public
- Voluntary

## Types of business organisation

Business organisations can take different forms. Regardless of the form of the organisation, one of the main reasons for being in business is to generate income and profits. This can be done by operating as a:

- sole trader
- partnership
- private limited company
- public limited company
- franchise.

### Sole trader

A typical sole trader shop

A **sole trader** is someone who owns the business on their own. They are responsible for the operation and running of the business. Examples of this type of business include local newsagents, hairdressers and tradespeople such as plumbers and electricians.

## Partnership

Coutts and Wylie is a partnership

A **partnership** is made up of at least two people (but less than 20) who are in business together. It is the preferred option for professionals such as accountants and lawyers and when they operate as a partnership they are allowed to have more than 20 partners. A partnership agreement is a legal document which is drawn up between the partners. It details how the partners will share profits and losses made in the business and how the business will operate, for example, who is responsible for what and so on.

## Limited companies

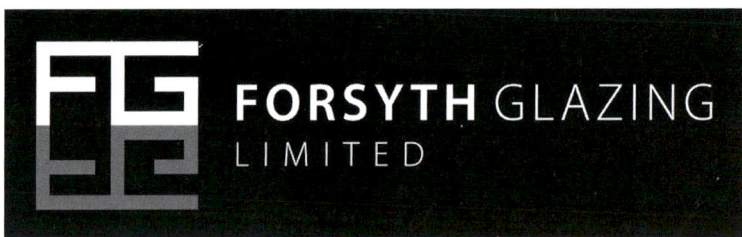

A **limited company** can be either private or public. It must have at least two **shareholders** who are the owners of the business. It is usually run by a board of directors who are responsible to the owners/shareholders of the business.

Private limited companies must have the word 'Limited' or the letters 'Ltd' after their name and they are not allowed to trade their shares on the stock market.

Public limited companies must have the letters 'plc' after their name and they are allowed to trade their shares on the stock market. Large companies like Stagecoach tend to operate as a plc.

All limited companies must register with the Registrar of Companies which is based at Companies House in Edinburgh – for Scottish companies. There are two main legal documents which apply to limited companies:

- Memorandum of Association which sets out the main aims of the business
- Articles of Association which describes how the business will operate and how it will be financed.

## Franchises

A **franchise** is a business which operates under the name of another business. The franchisee pays to operate with the business name and sells the products and services associated with the business name. Examples of successful franchises are McDonalds Restaurants and The Body Shop.

## Public sector organisations

**Public sector** organisations are owned and operated by the government on behalf of the public. Hospitals (NHS) are an example of this type of organisation. The government appoints people to run the organisation.

## Voluntary sector

Organisations in the **voluntary sector** are in business to provide a service or raise money. They are not in business to make a profit. Their aim is to maximise their potential to provide services through raising funds which are then used to further the cause. Charities such as Oxfam and Help the Aged are examples of voluntary organisations. A charity is the most common form of voluntary organisation in the UK.

In order to be recognised as a charity, an organisation must meet certain criteria. It must have at least one of the following as its main objective:

- To relieve poverty.
- To advance/promote education.
- To advance/promote religion.
- To carry out activities that benefit the community.

Organisations which have been granted charitable status are exempt from paying VAT.

### Revision tasks

1. State the minimum number of shareholders in a Limited Company.
2. State where shares are sold for a plc.
3. Identify the most common voluntary organisation in the UK.
4. Compare a sole trader with a partnership.
5. Compare a private limited company with a voluntary organisation.
6. Describe the term 'franchise'.

# Advantages and disadvantages of different types of business organisation

| Business type | Advantages | Disadvantages |
|---|---|---|
| Sole trader | ■ Easy to set up and operate.<br>■ Owner makes all the decisions. | ■ Owner has to take all responsibility – may involve long working hours.<br>■ Owner has unlimited liability. |
| Partnership | ■ Workload and responsibility can be shared.<br>■ More money invested since there are more owners in the business. | ■ Partners have unlimited liability.<br>■ Partners may leave and upset the operation of the business. |
| Private limited company | ■ Shareholders have limited liability.<br>■ Capital (money) can be raised from selling shares in the business. | ■ Financial information must be provided to the Registrar of Companies and is available to the public.<br>■ Larger organisations can be more difficult to run. |
| Public limited company | ■ Shares can be traded on the stock exchange. | ■ Same reasons as private limited companies. |
| Franchise | ■ Business benefits from established reputation.<br>■ Economies of scale, e.g. advertising.<br>■ Share good ideas. | ■ Franchisee is usually told exactly how to run the business.<br>■ Franchisee can only purchase supplies from franchiser.<br>■ Franchiser is usually entitled to some of the profit made. |
| Charity/voluntary | ■ Provide a worthwhile service.<br>■ Tax breaks from the government. | ■ Sometimes dependent on the support of individuals/local community. |

## Revision tasks

1. State two advantages of a partnership.
2. State one disadvantage of being a sole trader.
3. State one advantage and one disadvantage of running a franchise.
4. State one advantage and one disadvantage of a limited company.

# Business objectives – reasons for being in business

Business organisations have different reasons for being in business. We call these **objectives**. An organisation's objectives can depend on different things:

- Type of business.
- Size of business.
- The competition.
- Type of goods or services that it provides.

The following table gives examples of different business objectives and their meanings. Some organisations will try to focus on one or two objectives whilst others may try to achieve as many as possible. This will be decided by the owners of the business.

| Objective | What it means |
|---|---|
| Profit maximisation | This is where the organisation aims to make as much money as possible. It can be difficult to achieve other objectives as well as this one. |
| Growth | This is where the organisation tries to grow larger and increase its share of the market in which it operates. It could try to do this by charging lower prices than its competitors to attract more customers. |
| Survival | This means to continue trading/operating. Smaller organisations may focus on this objective. This is to avoid being taken over by other businesses and to continue to operate in their own right. |
| Social responsibility | This objective is increasingly important for the image of an organisation in the modern world. Customers wish to know that the business is responsible in its attitude to the environment or that it gives money to good causes. Although this may impact on the profits that the business is able to generate in the shorter term, it will ultimately benefit the business in the longer term. |
| Be 'green' (environmental awareness) | Many organisations now aim to reduce their 'carbon footprint' and display a 'green' image to their customers. This is likely to become more important in the future. Although this may cost the business money, it is likely to enable it to generate more profits to offset the additional costs. It also allows the business to be seen as 'socially responsible'. |
| Providing a service | This applies to most publicly funded organisations where their main aim is to provide a service that people require, e.g. hospitals. |

## Revision tasks

1. Outline two business objectives that might be followed by a private limited company and state the reasons why it might decide to follow them.
2. Outline the benefits to an organisation of following a 'green' agenda.
3. Outline a business objective that might be followed by a voluntary organisation.

SOC 4-20b

# What is a stakeholder?

A **stakeholder** can be defined as a person or group of people (an organisation) who are interested in how successful an organisation is. They exist in all different types and sizes of organisations.

The most common stakeholders of an organisation are:

| Private sector organisations | Public sector organisations | Voluntary sector organisations |
|---|---|---|
| Shareholders/owners | Board of directors | Board of trustees |
| Board of directors | Taxpayer | Donors |
| Employees | Suppliers | Recipients |
| Customers | | |
| Suppliers | | |
| Local community | | |
| Banks/lenders | | |
| The government | | |

Each stakeholder will have a different **interest** in the organisation and will be able to **influence** what it does in different ways. Be careful, because interest and influence are different things:

- **Interest** – the reasons why a stakeholder takes an interest in what the organisation is doing.
- **Influence** – the actions that the stakeholder can take that will impact upon the organisation and what it is doing.

## Revision tasks

1. Identify three stakeholders for a private sector organisation.
2. Identify three stakeholders for a public sector organisation.
3. Identify three stakeholders for a voluntary sector organisation.
4. Describe what is meant by stakeholder interest.
5. Describe what is meant by stakeholder influence.

# Private sector stakeholders

Examples include sole traders, partnerships and limited companies.

| Stakeholder | Who are they? | What interest do they have? | What influence do they have? |
|---|---|---|---|
| Shareholders/owners | - The people who have invested **capital** into a business.<br>- **Shareholders** are the owners of a limited company; they have bought **shares** in it.<br>- If the business is a sole trader or partnership, the person(s) who started the business with their own money will be the owner(s). | - Receive money in the form of profit or if they are a shareholder, through **dividends**. | - Shareholders of a company have voting rights which enable them to have a say in the way the company is run.<br>- If the organisation is a sole trader or partnership, the owner(s) will make all the decisions affecting the business. |
| Board of directors | - These are the individuals who are employed to manage and run the organisation. | - Receive payment for their work in the form of a **salary**. They may also receive other benefits such as a company car, bonuses, or private healthcare etc. | - Make the decisions that affect the organisation in the long term. These decisions will include what to produce (strategic decisions). |
| Employees | - Employees are the people who work for an organisation; they provide the physical and mental labour the organisation requires to function. | - Will receive a wage or salary for the work they do. They may also receive other benefits and 'perks'. They also expect to be treated fairly. | - Can participate in various forms of **industrial action** (e.g. strikes, work-to-rule, go slow) if they are unhappy at work. |
| Customers | - These are the people who purchase and consume the goods or services that an organisation provides. | - Because they have to spend their money on purchasing goods or services, they expect them to be of a good quality. They also expect to receive good customer service from the organisation. | - If a customer is unhappy, they can decide not to purchase from the organisation and to shop elsewhere (i.e. from a competitor). |
| Suppliers | - Provide organisations with the resources that they need to operate. These resources could be anything from raw materials to stationery to cleaning services. | - Interested in receiving orders from the organisation for the products that they provide. They also expect to be paid for the product that they have sold to the organisation. | - Can change the price of the product they sell, the delivery terms and any period of credit that may be given. |
| Local community | - These are the people who live near to where the organisation operates. | - Interested in the jobs that may be provided by the organisation as well as any negative impact it may have on the local area. This could be through pollution, noise or increased traffic. | - Can protest if they are unhappy at what the organisation is doing or they could complain to their MP (Member of Parliament). |
| Banks/lenders **RBS** The Royal Bank of Scotland | - Banks and other lenders provide organisations with loans and other sources of finance that the organisation may need (e.g. mortgage or overdraft). | - Want to make sure they are repaid the money that they have given the organisation on time and in accordance with the conditions laid down. | - Can refuse to offer the organisation additional finance and can change the rate of interest payable on any loan and the period of time the loan is taken out. |
| The government | - Responsible for providing the country with essential services such as health, education and defence. At a local level, e.g. Glasgow City Council, provides schools, roads, leisure facilities and refuse collection. | - Wants to make sure that jobs are provided to people in the country to maximise the money they receive from the organisation and its employees through taxation. | - Can change the amount of tax that is payable by an organisation. Can introduce or change the law which means the organisation may have to change what it is doing. Can also grant or refuse planning permission for the organisation to build new premises. |

SOC 4-20b

## Public sector organisations

Examples include public corporations, local government and central government.

| Stakeholder | Who are they? | What interest do they have? | What influence do they have? |
|---|---|---|---|
| Board of directors | ■ These are the individuals who are employed to manage and run the organisation on behalf of the government.<br>■ Accountable to the government. | ■ Receive payment for their work in the form of a salary. They may also receive other benefits such as a company car, bonuses, private healthcare etc. | ■ Make the decisions that will affect the organisation in the long term (strategic decisions). |
| Taxpayer | ■ These are members of the public who provide the government with money through their wages or by consuming (buying) goods/services. | ■ Interested in where their money goes and what they get in return for paying tax. | ■ Can complain to their MP if they are unhappy with the services provided by the government. |
| Suppliers | ■ Suppliers provide organisations with the resources that they need to operate. These resources could be anything from raw materials to stationery to cleaning services. | ■ Interested in receiving orders from the organisation for the products that they provide.<br>■ Expect to be paid for the product that they have sold to the organisation. | ■ Can change the price of the product they sell, the delivery terms and any period of credit that may be given. |

## Voluntary sector organisations

Examples include charities and voluntary sports clubs.

| Stakeholder | Who are they? | What interest do they have? | What influence do they have? |
|---|---|---|---|
| Board of trustees | ■ These are the people who manage and govern the way a voluntary organisation, e.g. a charity, will be run. | ■ Interested in ensuring the charity or organisation achieves its aims and that revenue generated from fundraising activities is spent in the best possible way. | ■ Make decisions that will impact upon the running of the organisation. |
| Donor | ■ People who donate money or other resources to the organisation. | ■ Want to make sure their donation is used in the best possible way. | ■ Can stop donating to the organisation or can change the level of support they give. |
| Recipient | ■ A person who benefits from the services provided by a voluntary organisation or support provided by a charity. | ■ Want to ensure the organisation provides them with the services or support they require. | ■ Could refuse to accept the services provided by the organisation or use it in an inappropriate way. |

## Revision tasks

1. Describe what is meant by a stakeholder.
2. Suggest three stakeholders of a private sector organisation.
3. Suggest three stakeholders of a public sector organisation.
4. Suggest three stakeholders of a voluntary organisation.
5. Suggest an interest of a supplier in an organisation.
6. Suggest an interest of an employee in an organisation.
7. Describe what is meant by a donor.
8. Describe what is meant by a taxpayer.
9. Suggest an influence a taxpayer has on an organisation.
10. Suggest an influence a manager has on an organisation.

## Activity

Choose two business organisations from the table below that you know or are interested in finding out about. Choose one from column A and one from column B. Visit the website for each business and use the Internet to find out any other relevant information before writing a short report on each. Your report should include the following:

- Name of the organisation.
- Number of employees.
- Name of person in charge.
- One other interesting fact that you have found out through your research.
- Type of organisation.
- Head office location.
- A short summary to describe the features and purpose of the business.

| Column A | | Column B | |
|---|---|---|---|
| McDonald's Restaurants<br>www.mcdonalds.co.uk | | Virgin Holidays<br>www.virginholidays.co.uk | |
| BT<br>www.bt.com | | Google<br>www.google.com | |
| Royal Mail<br>www.royalmail.com | | Thomson Holidays<br>www.thomson.co.uk | |
| Oxfam<br>www.oxfam.org.uk | | British Red Cross<br>www.redcross.org.uk | |

SOC 4-20b

29

### Activity

Choose a franchise that you are familiar with (e.g. McDonalds, Burger King, Pizza Hut) and find out what steps you would need to take to open up your own franchise. (You will find information to help you on the organisation's website.) Create a step-by-step guide.

### Activity

Many business organisations are finding new ways of trying to be seen as environmentally friendly and socially responsible. Choose an organisation and find out what they are doing to reduce carbon emissions and to increase the level of recycling that they are doing. Create a poster showing your findings.

### Activity

Choose two different types of organisation from the table on p. 29 and using your ICT skills, prepare a short presentation on:

- The stakeholders of the organisation.
- The interest the stakeholders have in the organisation.
- Examples of how different stakeholders have influenced the organisation.

### Web links

You may find it useful to visit the following websites for more information about business organisations:

- www.thetimes100.co.uk
- www.bized.co.uk
- www.bbc.co.uk/learning
- www.businessstudiesonline.co.uk

### Links to other subjects

In Personal and Social Education you learn about different types of organisations such as those that provide support to people in need or who provide essential services to the community. For example, you may have learned about the Samaritans and the services that they provide. This is an example of a voluntary organisation which has various stakeholders who may be interested in what the organisation is doing and how it is spending the money it receives through donations.

By studying Business at National 4 or Business Management at National 5/Higher you will learn more about different types of organisations and how they operate.

### What this means

**Business objectives** the targets or aims an organisation has.

**Capital** the money invested into a business by its owner(s).

**Dividend** an amount of money shareholders get back from the profits of an organisation in which they have invested.

**Industrial action** action taken by employees who are unhappy at work.

**Limited company** a company owned by shareholders.

**Partnership** a business owned by between two and twenty people.

**Private sector** organisations aiming to make a profit.

**Public sector** organisations aiming to provide a service. Owned by the government.

**Salary** a monthly payment a person receives for working in a company.

**Share** a unit of the value of a company. If the company is worth £100 and there are 10 shares then each share is worth £10.

**Shareholder** a person who has bought shares in a company.

**Sole trader** a business owned by one person.

**Stakeholder** a stakeholder can be defined as a person or group of people (an organisation) who are interested in how successful an organisation is.

**Voluntary sector** organisations aiming to help others or a particular cause.

# SOC 4–20c

## Definition of outcome — SOC 4–20c

I can evaluate working practices available to employees within different types of business organisations.

## Introduction to outcome

This outcome introduces you to the various working practices that are available to employees within a business organisation.

After working through this outcome you will be able to:

- describe what is meant by the term working practices
- identify different types of working practices commonly adopted by business organisations
- describe different types of working practices commonly adopted by business organisations
- describe the advantages of different types of working practices
- describe the disadvantages of different types of working practices
- evaluate the impact and effects of different types of working practices on a business organisation and its employees.

(There are lots of new business terms in this outcome. At the end of this outcome you will find a 'What this means' section to help you understand these new words.)

## Development of outcome

**Working practices** is a term that you have probably came across before, but what does it actually mean? It means the various ways employees can choose to work and includes where and when they can choose to work.

In a modern digital society, organisations no longer require or desire to have their employees working the traditional 9a.m. to 5p.m. Technology has enabled employees to work at a time and place of their choosing including at home or 'on the go'. Changes in the way businesses work and the different types of businesses that exist, has meant that employers and employees have more flexibility in when they can work. There are more businesses operating now that belong to the tertiary sector (and offer services around the clock) compared to more traditional businesses in the primary and secondary sectors.

Employees:

- can work **full-time** or **part-time**
- may be able to use technology to allow them to work on a **homeworking** or **teleworking** basis
- might work on a **job-share** basis
- might be allowed to choose their own start and finish times if their employer allows **flexitime**
- can be employed on a **permanent**, **temporary** or **fixed-term** basis.

| Full-time | This means someone will usually work between 35 and 40 hours per week. This could be 9a.m.–5p.m. five days a week or depending on the needs of the organisation, might involve working a number of shifts per week. |
|---|---|
| Part-time | This means someone will work less than 35 hours per week. They might work a couple of days per week, or they might work several afternoons and/or mornings per week. |
| Homeworking | As the title suggests, this means that the employee can work from home. They use technology (e.g. laptop and the Internet) to communicate with the office on a regular basis. They might work from home all the time, or only a couple of days per week. |
| Teleworking | Teleworking involves an employee working outwith the office and usually 'on the go'. They might use different pieces of technology e.g. a **personal digital assistant** (PDA) and/or laptop to communicate with the office. |
| Job-share | Job-share happens when two people are sharing one full-time job. This essentially means that one full-time job is being carried out by two people who are each working on a part-time basis. |
| Flexitime | Some organisations allow their employees to be flexible in their start and finish times. For example, they might be allowed to come into the office anytime between 9a.m. and 10a.m. and can finish anytime between 5p.m. and 6p.m. It enables employees to juggle their other commitments. |

## Contract of employment

When someone starts working for an organisation, they will be issued with a **contract of employment**. A contract is an agreement between two parties (i.e. employee and employer) that states the terms and conditions on which the person is being employed. The contract will state whether or not the employee is being employed on a permanent, temporary or fixed-term basis.

| Permanent | A permanent contract has no end date. The employee will be employed for as long as the job exists or until they leave the job or are **dismissed**. |
|---|---|
| Temporary | A temporary contract has no end date but the employee knows the job will not last for a long period of time. Usually temporary contracts allow organisations to cope with any periods of time where the work load has increased (e.g. perhaps to cover busy periods over Christmas or the summer). |
| Fixed-term | Fixed-term contracts cover a specific period of time e.g. a few months or a year. When the employee starts a job on a fixed-term basis they know in advance when the employment will come to an end. |

There are many advantages and disadvantages of different working practices for both the organisation and employee.

### Advantages to an organisation
- Employees can be more motivated meaning that they will work harder and be more productive (this in turn could mean less employees take days off work 'sick' and a lower staff turnover).
- Unexpected changes in demand can be managed more easily.
- Money can be saved if less space in offices is required to accommodate employees as they can work away from the office.

### Disadvantages to an organisation
- Technology could be expensive to purchase and maintain for employees who are homeworkers or teleworkers.
- Employees require training to use technology which could be expensive and working time is lost when employees are being trained.
- Some employees may not want to use technology and could resist change.

### Advantages to an employee
- Other commitments (e.g. children) can be managed more easily.
- Money can be saved as less travelling maybe required.
- Higher job satisfaction and motivation and less stress.

**Disadvantages to an employee**
- Some working practices may not suit the employee.
- The employee might not want to use technology or might feel pressured into using it.

### Summary

Different working practices enable both the employer and employee to manage better their workload and changes that occur in the business environment.

### Revision tasks

1. Describe each type of working practice.
2. Describe the difference between a temporary and fixed-term contract.
3. Describe two advantages of flexible working practices for an organisation.
4. Describe two advantages of flexible working practices for an employee.

### Activity

Do some Internet research to find out about flexible working practices that different organisations offer. Remember, that not every organisation will offer every type of working practice!

Or even better, if you know someone who works for an organisation that has flexible working practices, you should ask them about their experiences and what they like/dislike about it.

### Activity

The government's Directgov website provides more information on flexible working practices, including whether or not you may be entitled to request it in accordance with the law. Find out more at:

www.direct.gov.uk/en/employment/employees/workinghoursandtimeoff/dg_10029491

SOC 4–20c

### Links to other subjects

Different working practices can enable employees to have a better life because they feel less stressed and happier at work. Stress at work can be a difficult thing for people to manage and sometimes they have to seek help and advice from their GP (General Practitioner) or from other agencies to help with this. You will learn about how to cope with stress (e.g. during exams) in Personal and Social Education and from your school.

If you choose to take Administration & IT at National 4 or National 5, you will learn more about working practices in the business environment. You will also learn more about the duties owed by employers to their employees.

### What this means

**Contract of employment** a formal, written agreement between employer and employee which states the terms and conditions of employment.

**Dismissed** employee no longer required for their job.

**Fixed-term** fixed-term contracts cover a specific period of time, e.g. a few months or a year.

**Flexitime** employees are given flexibility in their start and finish times, but usually have to be at work during 'core times'.

**Full-time** this means someone will usually work between 35 and 40 hours per week.

**Homeworking** the employee can work from home using technology to assist them with their work.

**Job-share** two people sharing one full-time job.

**Part-time** this means someone will work less than 35 hours per week.

**Permanent** a permanent contract has no end date.

**Personal digital assistant (PDA)** a handheld portable device that allows people to enter appointments and organise themselves.

**Teleworking** teleworking involves an employee working outwith the office and usually 'on the go'.

**Temporary** a contract with no end date but the employee knows the job will not last for a long period of time.

**Working practices** the various ways employees can choose to work and includes where and when they work.

# 6

# SOC 4–21a

## Definition of outcome — SOC 4–21a

I can evaluate the suitability of finance options available for setting up and supporting different types of businesses.

## Introduction to outcome

This outcome is focused on business organisations and the money (or finance) that is required to set them up and support them. Business organisations may be public, private or voluntary in nature. We will consider different sources of finance and their suitability to different types of businesses.

After working through this outcome you will be able to:

- describe the features of different types of finance available to different business organisations:
    - overdraft
    - trade credit
    - hire purchase
    - capital
    - bank loan
    - mortgage
    - debenture
    - grants
    - European Union funds
    - other forms of government assistance
- describe the suitability of different types of finance for different business purposes
- evaluate the suitability of different finance options and match them to different situations.

## Development of outcome

Business organisations are part of our everyday lives. We have considered different types of businesses in outcome SOC 4–20b and categorised them as belonging to one of three sectors of business, private, public or voluntary.

Within these different categories, we identified businesses as one of the following types:

- Sole trader.
- Partnership.
- Private/public limited company.
- Franchise.

All businesses, regardless of type, require money (finance) to set up and continue operating over time. The type of finance that they might consider will be influenced by two factors:

- What the money is needed for.
- The type of organisation they are.

Most organisations will have access to two different sources of finance. Money saved from profits made by a business in previous years is an example of an **internal** source of finance. This is a very important source of finance because there is no cost attached to it.

All other sources of finance are considered to be **external**. This means that they are provided by someone else in the form of a type of loan to the business. The cost of borrowing different amounts of money for different periods of time will vary. External sources of finance are usually listed as being either short term or long term.

> **What this means**
>
> **Internal**
> this means within the organisation and is something over which the business will probably have control.
>
> **External**
> this means outwith the organisation and is something over which the business will not have control.

## Short term

Short-term sources of finance are normally due to be paid back within 3 years or less. Here are some examples:

| Short-term source of finance/definition | Advantages | Disadvantages |
|---|---|---|
| **Overdraft** This is a short-term loan provided by the bank on your account. | This is usually agreed in advance and many organisations will arrange a permanent overdraft facility. | It can cost a lot of money over a short period of time and it is normally repayable on demand. |
| **Short-term loan** As it says it is a short-term loan usually provided by a bank for a specific purpose. | This is agreed in advance and will normally have a fixed interest rate and fixed repayments which will not change over the period of the loan. | The full amount borrowed plus interest set by the bank has to be repaid. |
| **Trade credit** This is where credit is offered by suppliers giving you more time to pay for goods/services. | Having trade credit can improve your cash flow – if you are able to sell the goods before you need to pay for them. | You need to monitor your cash flow carefully and manage your creditors. Also, your customers may expect to receive the same credit terms from you. |
| **Hire purchase** This is where assets are purchased by paying equal instalments of the cost plus interest over an agreed period of time. | The cost is spread over a set period of time and the repayment amounts are fixed. This helps with budgeting. | You do not have legal title (i.e. you do not own the assets) until the last payment has been made. |

## Long term

Long-term sources of finance are normally due to be paid back over a period of more than 3 years. Here are some examples:

| Long-term source of finance/definition | Advantages | Disadvantages |
|---|---|---|
| **Capital** <br> This is where the amount of money invested in the business is increased by the owners/shareholders. | The business does not need to pay back the amount of money invested and there is no interest/cost. | Profits may need to be shared out amongst more people if there are more investors. |
| **Long-term loan** <br> As it says it is a long-term loan usually provided by a bank for a specific purpose. | This is agreed in advance and will normally have a fixed interest rate and fixed repayments which will not change over the period of the loan. | The full amount borrowed plus interest set by the bank has to be repaid. |
| **Mortgage** <br> This is a loan which is usually secured against property and will normally be for a large amount of money. | Repayments are made in regular fixed instalments so it is good for budgeting and planning. | The amount borrowed has to be repaid plus interest. The rate of interest may go up or down depending on the type of deal that is agreed. |
| **Debenture** <br> This is a type of loan which is usually secured on the assets of the business and will normally be for a large amount of money. It is only available to public limited companies. | The rate of interest charged on the debenture is usually fixed over the period of the loan and this is paid until the loan amount becomes repayable at a fixed date in the future. | The interest on the debenture must be repaid before any dividends are paid to shareholders. The amount borrowed has to be repaid plus interest. |

## Government assistance

Help and assistance may also be available from the government, particularly for starting up a new business. Here are some examples:

| Source of assistance/definition | Advantages | Disadvantages |
|---|---|---|
| **Grant** <br> This is money provided for a specific purpose or project but will not normally cover the entire cost. | It does not usually need to be repaid. | May have conditions attached. Might not get the amount asked for. |
| **European Union funds** <br> Money may be available in the form of grants or loans from different European funding sources. | Grants may not need to be repaid and loans may be offered at a low rate of interest. | Loans will still need to be repaid plus interest. |

Table continued on next page...

| Source of assistance/definition | Advantages | Disadvantages |
|---|---|---|
| **Enterprise Finance Guarantee** <br> This is where the government guarantees that a business will be able to repay money that it borrows. | Makes it easier for new businesses to borrow money. | The full amount borrowed plus interest has to be repaid. <br><br> Only available until 31 March 2011. |
| **Reduced corporation tax for small businesses** <br> As the name suggests, lower rates of tax are available to small businesses. | Small businesses are required to pay less corporation tax than larger businesses. | Some tax still needs to be paid to the government on the profits made. |
| **Government advice and assistance** <br> A variety of support and advice is available to help new and existing businesses. | This assistance is usually free of charge. | None |
| **Prince's Trust** <br> Provides practical and financial support to young people starting up in business. | Free advice. | May not be suited to all types of business. |
| **Business Gateway** <br> Practical help, advice and support for new and growing businesses in Scotland. <br> www.bgateway.com | Free advice and support. | Available to new and growing businesses. |

## Revision tasks

1. Outline the differences between a short-term loan and an overdraft.
2. Outline one advantage and one disadvantage of hire purchase as a source of finance.
3. Define the term long-term finance.
4. List two examples of long-term finance.
5. Compare a mortgage with a long-term bank loan.
6. List an example of a free source of finance.
7. Outline one form of government assistance.

## Activity

Familiarise yourself with each of the organisations listed in the table below by visiting their websites and carrying out some research. Beside each of the organisations listed in the table, there is a finance requirement. You are required to identify the following in a short report for each organisation:

- The type of business.
- A source of finance that would be suitable to meet the requirement.
- One advantage of the source of finance identified.
- One disadvantage of the source of finance identified.
- A reason why the source of finance identified is suitable for the purpose required.

| Organisation | | Finance requirement |
|---|---|---|
| Royal Mail www.royalmail.com | | A fleet of new delivery vans |
| BT www.bt.com | | More capital |
| Oxfam www.oxfam.org.uk | | New photocopiers for Head Office |
| Google www.google.com | | A new head office building |

## Links to other subjects

There are lots of opportunities for you to learn about financial management across the curriculum, for example in Numeracy and Maths and also in Personal & Social Education. If your school offers Financial Education then this will also allow you to learn more.

If you choose to take Business or Lifeskills Mathematics at National 4, you will learn more about financial management. Accounting at National 5 will also provide you with the opportunity to learn more about financial management.

## What this means

**Internal** this means within the organisation and is something over which the business will probably have control.

**External** this means outwith the organisation and is something over which the business will not have control.

# SOC 4–21b

## Definition of outcome — SOC 4–21b

Having considered the financial needs of individuals and businesses, I can evaluate, prepare and present financial information and documents to assist in making appropriate financial decisions.

## Introduction to outcome

This outcome is concerned with how financial information is used by individuals and businesses. It links in with outcome MNU 3–09b and focuses on the following aspects:

- what is a bank?
- Internet banking
- bank statements
- budgeting/money management
- debit/credit cards
- responsible lending.

After working through this outcome you will be able to:

- describe the purpose of a bank
- describe what Internet banking is
- describe the main parts of a bank statement
- explain why budgeting is important
- describe what is meant by a debit and credit card
- understand the need for responsible lending.

## Development of outcome

### What is a bank?

**What this means**

**Bank**
a provider of financial services and bank accounts.

A **bank** is a company that will look after your money. Common banks you will find on your high street include Lloyds TSB, Bank of Scotland, The Royal Bank of Scotland, Clydesdale Bank and NatWest.

**RBS** *The Royal Bank of Scotland*

You can put your money into a **bank account** and the bank will store it safely until you wish to spend it. When you open a bank account, you are given a bank account number and usually a card so that you can get access to your money – sometimes at a cash machine (ATM) using a special PIN (Personal Identification Number) that only you should know.

### What this means

**Bank account**
a facility offered by a bank whereby a person can credit (put in) money and debit (withdraw) money.

Banks also offer a range of other services including mortgages, business banking and loans.

## Internet banking

Most banks now let you access your bank account and other services online. This is known as **Internet banking**. Using a username and password you can log into the bank's website and find out how much money you have in your account, and you can transfer it to other accounts (e.g. to pay bills). This makes life much easier to manage your money as it can be accessed at any time; you don't need to wait until the bank is open to access Internet banking.

### What this means

**Internet banking**
an online facility provided by a bank that enables users to check and use their bank account at any time.

## Bank statements

At the end of each month, you will receive a **bank statement** that shows how much money you have put into your account and how much money has been taken from your account. It then shows a final balance showing how much you have left.

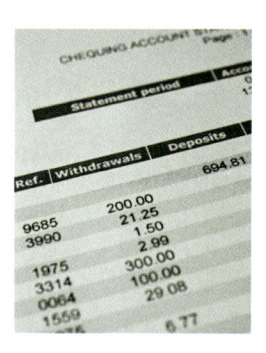

### What this means

**Bank statement**
a document showing how money has gone in and gone out of a bank account over a period of time (usually 1 month).

## What this means

**Budget**
a plan (or forecast) of how much money will be received and spent over a period of time.

## Budgeting

You need to plan carefully to manage the money you have coming in and going out; this is known as **budgeting** or money management. It is important to do this to make sure you don't spend more than you actually have.

At the beginning of the month you should make a list of all the money you have coming in (this is known as receipts) for example:

>   Pocket money £10
>   
>   Money from paper round £20
>   
>   **Total receipts = £30**

You can then decide how much you wish to spend. With a budget of £30, a person who budgets very carefully will only spend up to £30 – you don't want to be asking your parents or friends for more money because you have spent too much!

Businesses usually prepare a budget for a few months at a time. This shows how much money they expect to have coming in from sales and how much money they expect to spend on other expenses (e.g. rent, heating, employee wages etc.). They might use a spreadsheet to help them prepare this.

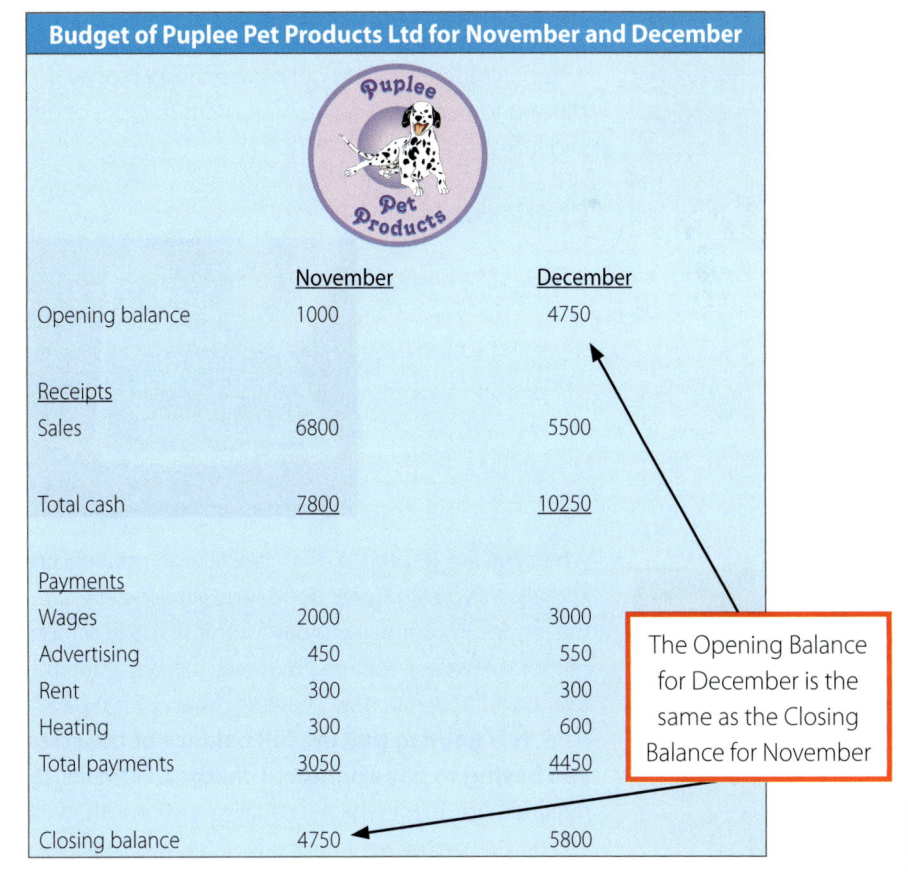

**Budget of Puplee Pet Products Ltd for November and December**

|  | November | December |
|---|---|---|
| Opening balance | 1000 | 4750 |
|  |  |  |
| Receipts |  |  |
| Sales | 6800 | 5500 |
|  |  |  |
| Total cash | 7800 | 10250 |
|  |  |  |
| Payments |  |  |
| Wages | 2000 | 3000 |
| Advertising | 450 | 550 |
| Rent | 300 | 300 |
| Heating | 300 | 600 |
| Total payments | 3050 | 4450 |
|  |  |  |
| Closing balance | 4750 | 5800 |

The Opening Balance for December is the same as the Closing Balance for November

The budget shows how much money the company expects to receive (receipts) and how much money it expects to spend (payments).

A budget is prepared in advance so that planning and decision making can take place.

## Debit and credit cards

### Debit cards

> **What this means**
>
> **Debit card**
> a card that enables you to pay for goods and services in a shop using a PIN. The bank account is checked.

When you are 16 years old, you are able to obtain a **debit card** from your bank. This allows you to pay for goods and services using the 'chip and PIN' facility offered by most shops and supermarkets. When you use your card to pay for something, your bank account is checked to make sure you have enough money to pay for your purchases. If you do not have enough money in your account, you will not be allowed to purchase your items. Common types of debit cards are Solo, Visa Debit and Maestro.

### Credit cards

> **What this means**
>
> **Credit card**
> a card that enables goods to be purchased 'on credit'. This means buying them now and paying for them later.

When you are 18 years old, you are able to obtain a **credit card** from your bank. This allows you to pay for goods and services, even though you might not have the money in your bank to pay for them. You buy them 'on credit' which means you pay for them later. You would usually receive a statement at the end of the month telling you how much you have spent and what payment you need to make to the bank. **It is good to pay the full balance of the statement in full – this avoids you having to pay additional charges.** However, the bank usually only asks for a minimum payment which is usually much less than what you have actually spent. If you only make the minimum payments, it will take longer to pay off the balance of your credit card and you will have to pay interest (charges) on this. Common types of credit cards are Visa, MasterCard and American Express.

A chip and PIN machine

You will see on many shop windows whether or not they accept debit and/or credit cards. You insert your card into the chip and PIN machine and type in your PIN number to pay for your purchases.

## Responsible lending

When you are 18, you are able to take advantage of a number of credit facilities offered by banks and other financial providers. These include loans, overdrafts and mortgages. Before deciding to give you any of these, the bank or provider will run a credit check on you to see whether or not you are a responsible customer and could afford to pay back these debts. They do this in line with their responsible lending policy. However, ultimately, the customer is responsible for their own debt and many people take out too much credit which can lead to stress, depression and other problems if they are unable to pay these debts back. It can also have severe long-term consequences on the individual in the future.

### Revision tasks

1. Describe what a bank is.
2. Name three banks.
3. Describe what is meant by a bank account.
4. Describe the purpose of a bank statement.
5. Give an advantage of Internet banking.
6. Describe what is meant by a budget.
7. How old do you have to be to obtain a debit card?
8. How old do you have to be to obtain a credit card?
9. Explain the difference between a debit and credit card.
10. Give two examples of a debit card.
11. Give two examples of a credit card.
12. Explain why banks have a policy of responsible lending.

## Activity

The Royal Bank of Scotland has a fantastic resource for 11–14 year olds to access to help them learn about money and financial education. Go onto the bank's website www.rbs.co.uk and search for 'MoneySense'. You should work through the tasks and activities on this for 11–14 year olds.

## Activity

Using your spreadsheet skills, create the budget you saw earlier in this chapter. Insert formulae where appropriate. Try changing the sales figure and the different expenses figures to see what the impact upon the closing balance for that month is.

### Links to other subjects

There are lots of opportunities for you to learn about budgeting and money management across the curriculum, for example in Numeracy and Maths and also in Personal & Social Education. You might also get the opportunity to use spreadsheets to create budgets in IT classes.

If you choose to take Business or Lifeskills Mathematics at National 4, you will learn more about financial management. Accounting at National 5 will also provide you with the opportunity to learn more about financial management.

## What this means

**Bank**  a provider of financial services and bank accounts.

**Bank account**  a facility offered by a bank whereby a person can credit (put in) money and debit (withdraw) money.

**Bank statement**  a document showing how money has gone in and gone out of a bank account over a period of time (usually 1 month).

**Budget**  a plan (or forecast) of how much money will be received and spent over a period of time.

**Credit card**  a card that enables goods to be purchased 'on credit'. This means buying them now and paying for them later.

**Debit card**  a card that enables you to pay for goods and services in a shop using a PIN. The bank account is checked.

**Internet banking**  an online facility provided by a bank that enables users to check and use their bank account at any time.

# SOC 4–22a

## Definition of outcome  — SOC 4–22a

By researching the organisation of a business, I can discuss the role of departments and personnel, evaluating how they contribute to the success or failure of the business.

## Introduction to outcome

This outcome is focused on business organisations, their structure and how they operate. This outcome also focuses on the people that help run the business and the parts that they play in making it all work.

In this outcome, we will focus on the structure and operation of a private limited company.

After working through this outcome you will be able to:

- describe the structure of an organisation
- describe the use of functional departments
- describe the advantages of functional departments
- describe the disadvantages of functional departments
- describe the activities of functional departments
- describe different forms of organisational structure
- distinguish between formal and informal structures
- describe factors affecting the internal structure of an organisation.

## Development of outcome

All organisations need to be organised. This generally means that they will be arranged into teams or departments. Structure means that they can work properly. Everyone who works in the organisation needs to know where they fit into the structure. For example:

- Who (people) and what (things) they are responsible for.
- Who (person) they are responsible to.

- What decisions (type and level) they can make.
- Where (to which person or place) they should go to for information.
- How they fit into the structure of the organisation as a whole.

### What this means

**Organisation chart** this shows the different levels of jobs, their titles and the names of the people who work in the organisation represented in a diagram.

Different organisations will be structured in different ways. We are going to use the example of a private limited company. It is a fictional company called Puplee Pet Products Ltd which manufactures a range of products for cats and dogs. The **organisation chart** looks like this:

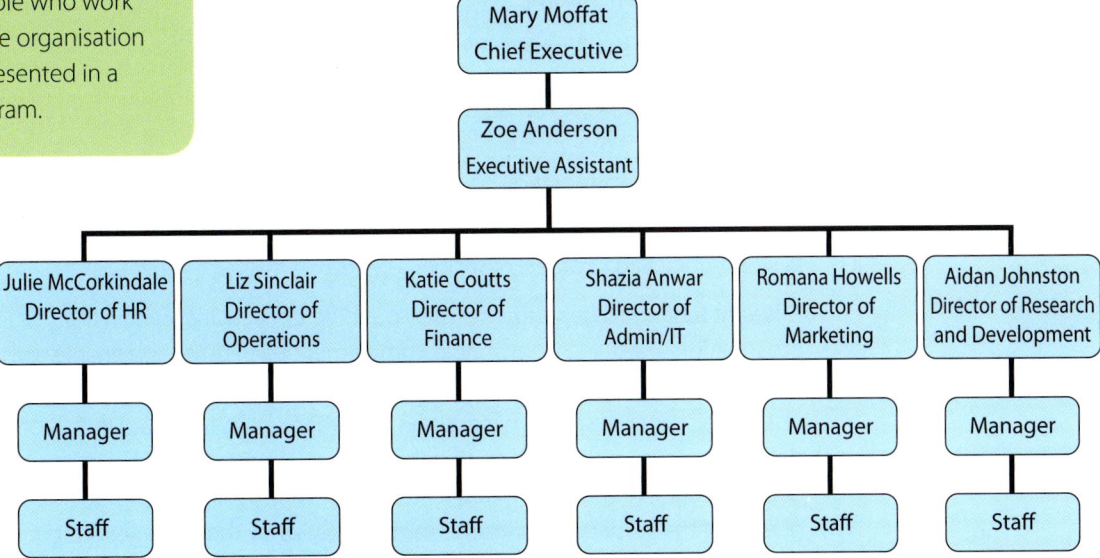

```
                    Mary Moffat
                   Chief Executive
                          |
                    Zoe Anderson
                  Executive Assistant
                          |
   ┌────────────┬─────────┼─────────┬────────────┬────────────┐
Julie         Liz        Katie    Shazia       Romana       Aidan
McCorkindale  Sinclair   Coutts   Anwar        Howells      Johnston
Director      Director   Director Director     Director     Director of
of HR         of         of       of           of           Research and
              Operations Finance  Admin/IT     Marketing    Development
   |            |           |         |            |             |
Manager      Manager     Manager   Manager      Manager       Manager
   |            |           |         |            |             |
 Staff        Staff       Staff     Staff        Staff         Staff
```

Mary Moffat is the Chief Executive and she is responsible to the Board of Directors for the day-to-day running of the organisation. There are six departments which are arranged round the functional activities of the organisation:

- Human Resources (HR)
- Operations
- Finance
- Administration/IT
- Marketing
- Research and Development (R&D).

Within each department there is a director in overall charge supported by at least one functional manager. Staff below management level within each department range in number from 10 to 80. The total staff complement is about 180.

SOC 4-22a

Different organisations can have different sizes of departments depending on their needs. In Puplee Pet Products Ltd, the biggest department is the Operations department. The smallest department is the human resources department.

The use of functional departments means that all the people in a certain department possess skills or experience in that particular area.

The main advantages of using functional departments are:

- better use of resources
- development of expertise in particular areas
- good routes of communication
- creation of career paths
- opportunities for people to work better together as part of a dedicated team
- better decision making.

The disadvantages of using functional departments are:

- a feeling amongst staff that they only work for the department/team that they are part of rather than the organisation as a whole
- departments cannot work in isolation as they need other departments to solve problems
- communication barriers may open up between departments.

Different functional departments carry out different activities within the organisation. These activities should complement each other and enable the departments to work collectively for the good of the organisation. It is the responsibility of the senior managers in the organisation to ensure that each department runs smoothly and that there is good communication between departments. In Puplee Pet Products Ltd, this responsibility lies with the directors of each of the six departments. They are supported by the managers within each of the departments.

### Human resources department

The human resources (HR) department is responsible for managing the staffing of the organisation. These responsibilities include hiring new staff (recruitment), providing staff training, carrying out staff appraisal and any other issues relating to staff welfare.

The staff in this department will usually have some knowledge of employment law and will be able to advise the organisation in this area.

> **Activity**
>
> Research and list the different activities carried out in the HR department of an organisation of your choice.

### Operations department

The operations department can be involved in different processes depending on the nature of the business that the organisation carries out. For example, this department can be responsible for the purchase and storage of raw materials, the production of the end product that the organisation sells, and the storage and distribution of the finished product.

> **Activity**
>
> Research and list the different activities carried out in the operations department of an organisation of your choice.

### Finance department

The finance department is responsible for maintaining and storing all the financial records of the business. They keep track of all financial transactions and the money coming into and going out of the business. One of its priorities is to maintain a good cash flow to ensure that the business keeps operating.

The finance department must produce reports and accounts for both internal and external use. Financial information used internally by the directors and managers is a form of management information and it is used for decision making. This department is also responsible for budgets and forecasts. These are essential to the future operation and planning of the business.

> **Activity**
>
> Research and list the different activities carried out in the finance department of an organisation of your choice.

SOC 4-22a

## Administration/IT department

The administration and information technology (IT) departments within organisations are often combined. This is because they are closely related and linking them together allows cost savings to be made.

The main function of administration is to ensure the smooth flow of information around the business and keep a record of what the business does. In the past, much of this work would have been done using manual systems without the use of computers. Since the use of computers and IT became more widespread in business, most administrative functions have become dependent on the use of IT. The work of the administration and IT departments have become closely related.

The main function of the IT department is to provide the organisation and its staff with IT support and a safe and secure environment in which to carry out their work. The use of IT in organisations has increased dramatically over the years and the safe and secure operation of this function is central to the day-to-day running of most organisations. This includes the operation and maintenance of computer systems, Internet, network, printers, all computer equipment and mobile communications.

### Activity

Research and list the different activities carried out in the administration or IT department of an organisation of your choice.

## Marketing department

This is perhaps the most important department in the organisation. Its main responsibility is to find out what consumers want (to buy). It finds this out by using market research methods. If their research is faulty then the organisation could produce the wrong product or service which no one will want to buy.

When the department has decided on the products to produce, it must then decide on the correct marketing mix. This is made up of the four 'Ps'. These are:

| | |
|---|---|
| Price | must be set at a level that consumers are willing to pay for the goods and also enable the organisation to make a profit. |
| Product | this must be what the consumers want and must do what they want it to do. |
| Place | the process by which the product reaches the market in the right place at the right time and in the right quantity. |
| Promotion | telling consumers about the product and enticing them to buy it through advertising and promotions. |

The marketing mix

Product • Price • Place • Promotion — Target Market

### What this means

**Budget** this is where future money coming in and out of the business is planned.

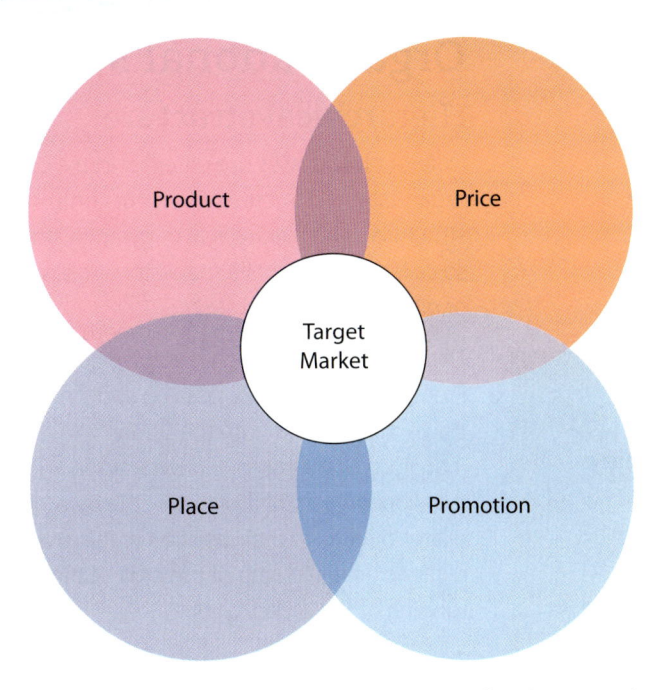

Marketing departments in large modern organisations often have very large **budgets** available to them in order that they can try to attract as many customers to their products as possible.

### Activity

Research and list the different activities carried out in the marketing department of an organisation of your choice.

## Research and development department

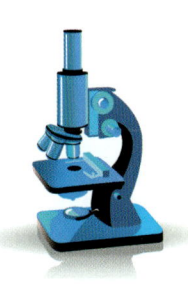

The research and development (R&D) department is in charge of developing new products and improving existing products. This department needs to work closely with the marketing department which will share market research information with it.

The size of the department will be determined by the size of the organisation and the types of products that it produces.

# Organisational structure

## Hierarchical structure

Different businesses use different forms of organisational structure. The most common structure is the hierarchical or pyramid structure, so called because of its shape. It contains lots of different layers.

This is the structure used in Puplee Pet Products Ltd. Decisions pass up and down the pyramid from the senior managers at the top of the pyramid to the workforce at the bottom of the pyramid. An individual's position on the pyramid relates directly to their position within the organisation i.e. those at the top of the pyramid are at the top of the organisation and have greater **responsibility** for the running of the organisation.

The different levels of the organisation represented on the levels of the pyramid relate to the different functional departments within the organisation. Staff within each functional department usually have experience and expertise in a particular area and this means they often become specialised in a particular role.

> **What this means**
>
> **Responsibility**
> those who are higher up in the organisation have more of an obligation to guide and control it.

### Disadvantages

**Procedures** must be arranged and followed to allow the departments and staff to communicate effectively as they are dependent on each other. Poor communication between staff and departments can lead to problems within the organisation. One result is that the organisation could become slow to react to change. Communication has to pass through each layer of the organisation which takes time and also means that information can be lost.

Decision making can also be adversely affected by this structure. If the information required to make decisions needs to be collected from different departments then this can take time and thus lead to poor decision making.

> **What this means**
>
> **Procedures**
> actions and operations that are set out for staff to follow when dealing with certain situations.

## Flat structure

Some organisations prefer to use a flat structure. As the name suggests, this is the opposite of a hierarchical structure and it has fewer layers of management. Fewer layers mean that there are fewer problems with communication, decision making and being able to react to changes from external pressures. In this style of structure it is also likely that the owner of the business will know all of the staff. The flat structure makes the organisation work as one team and allows a better response to change than the hierarchical structure.

```
            Flat
          structure
  ┌────┬────┬────┬────┬────┬────┐
  □    □    □    □    □    □
```

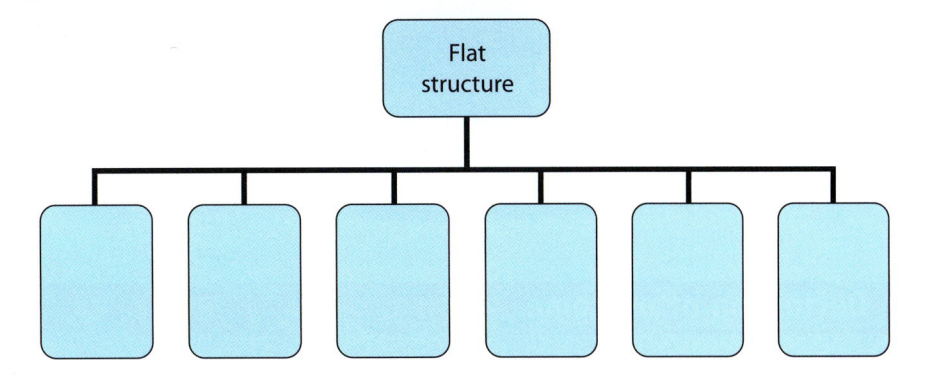

When organisations change from a hierarchical structure to a flat structure it is called delayering.

## Activity

1. Identify the departments in your school.
2. Is there an organisation chart available for your school?
3. Does your school have a hierarchical or a flat structure?
4. List three pieces of useful information that can be taken from an organisation chart.
5. List the advantages to Puplee Pet Products Ltd of changing from a hierarchical structure to a flat structure.
6. Explain how a change in structure could affect decision making in the organisation.

### What this means

**Budget** this is where future money coming in and out of the business is planned.

**Organisation chart** this shows the different levels of jobs, their titles and the names of the people who work in the organisation represented in a diagram.

**Procedures** actions and operations that are set out for staff to follow when dealing with certain situations.

**Responsibility** those who are higher up in the organisation have more of an obligation to guide and control it.

# SOC 4–22b

## Definition of outcome — SOC 4–22b

I can identify internal and external factors influencing planning and decision making and can assess how these decisions contribute to the success or failure of a business.

## Introduction to outcome

This outcome looks at the different factors and issues that can impact upon business when decisions are being made. This links in with outcome SOC 4–20a Economic factors.

After working through this outcome you will be able to:

- describe what decision making is
- identify different levels of decision making
- describe different levels of decision making
- identify the internal factors that impact and influence decision making
- explain the internal factors that impact and influence decision making
- identify the external factors that impact and influence decision making
- explain the external factors that impact and influence decision making.

(There are lots of new business terms in this outcome. At the end of this outcome you will find a 'What this means' section to help you understand these new words.)

## Development of outcome

### What is decision making?

**Decision making** takes place at all levels of organisations and involves choosing one option from a range of options. Decision making is important because it drives the direction of the organisation and what will happen in the future. When organisations are planning ahead and thinking about what product to make, what price to charge and where to sell their product, they are making decisions. If these decisions are wrongly made, this could have serious consequences for the success of the organisation.

## Types of decisions

### Strategic
These are long-term decisions that affect the overall direction of the company. They are made by managers at the highest level.

### Tactical
These are medium-term decisions that are the stepping stones to achieving strategic decisions. They are made by middle level managers.

### Operational
These are short-term decisions that impact upon an organisation on a daily basis. They are made by low level managers.

## Internal factors

When decisions are being made, management have to consider a range of internal and external factors. Internal factors are things within an organisation. These include the following.

### Finance

The level of finance available to support a decision will impact upon the decision that can be made. The finance being invested in a particular decision should be justifiable in terms of the benefits it brings.

### Information

The information available should be of a high quality and relevant to the decision being made. Wrong information could lead to wrong decisions being made.

## Technology

Technology can be used to model and test the impact of different decisions. Businesses can use this technology to see 'what if' scenarios if certain paths were chosen. Technology can also be used (such as spreadsheets) to analyse statistics and construct graphs. Formulae can also be used in spreadsheets to forecast and predict the financial outcome of certain decisions.

## Skills of management

Managers who have been trained in decision making are more likely to make better decisions compared to those who have not. Those who have had experience of making decisions are in a more informed position to be able to make similar decisions.

## External factors

External factors are those things outwith the control of an organisation that impact upon its activities and decision making. The best way to remember these is by using the acronym PESTEC.

### Political

Political factors – actions the government takes and how this impacts on business. For example, changing laws and regulations.

## Economic

Economic factors – what is happening in the business world that impacts on how much the business can buy and sell. For example, changing demand, changing taxes, changing interest rates and the impact of a recession.

## Social

Social factors – the changing tastes and preferences of consumers. For example, the changing demands of consumers with respect to fashion.

## Technological

Technological factors – the introduction and availability of new technology. More advanced and sophisticated technology can enable a business to do new things and to change the way it operates. For example – the introduction of self-service checkouts at supermarkets.

## Environmental

Environmental factors – issues to do with the environment that must be considered. Businesses today are required to act and behave in a much more socially responsive way. They need to be seen to promote 'green issues' and participate in recycling, reduce carbon omissions and other environmental practices.

SOC 4–22b

## Competition

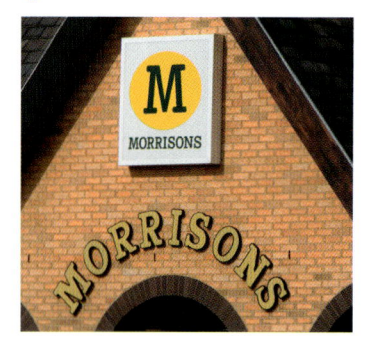

Competition factors – the actions of other similar businesses in the market place. The decisions that are being made by competitors have an impact upon the decisions made by a company. If a competitor changes its price or product, this needs to be considered in the decision-making process.

### Summary

Decision making takes place at all levels of an organisation and takes place all the time. In order to make the best decisions, managers have to consider a number of factors (internal and external) to ensure that they make the best one.

### Revision tasks

1. Identify the three levels of decision making.
2. Suggest who makes strategic decisions.
3. Suggest who makes operational decisions.
4. Explain why the availability of finance is important in decision making.
5. Identify the acronym that can be used to remember different external factors.
6. Describe what is meant by the different external factors.

### Activity

In groups, choose one of the external factors – PESTEC – and investigate how this could impact upon business. Present your findings in a method of your choice (e.g. presentation, website, report, magazine article or poster) to the rest of your class.

### Activity

Imagine you are the managing director of an airline. What measures could you introduce to reduce wastage on your aeroplanes and in your company? Make a list of these.

### Activity

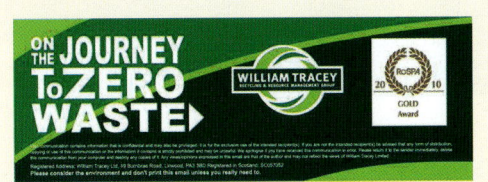

The William Tracey Group, based in Linwood (Paisley), is now a leading recycling company in the UK. However, it began its life as a skip hire company and has changed the way that it operates to meet customer demand and to keep up with the changing external business environment. Access the William Tracey Group website (www.williamtraceygroup.com) and write down all of the different activities that it is now involved in.

### Links to other subjects

In Modern Studies and/or Politics you will consider the different laws and policies of different political parties; these could impact upon business in different ways.

In Personal and Social Education you will look at different environmental issues including litter, recycling, carbon emissions and behaving ethically. Think about how these issues apply to and affect business.

In Administration & IT and Computing & Information Science (at National 4 and 5), you will look at the impact of new technology on individuals and you should consider the way that this could impact upon business.

Business at National 4 and Business Management at National 5 will explore external influences in much greater depth.

### What this means

**Decision making** choosing one option from a range of choices.

**External factors** things outwith an organisation that impact on how it operates.

**Internal factors** things within an organisation that impact on how it operates.

**Operational** these are short-term decisions that impact on an organisation on a daily basis. They are made by low level managers.

**Strategic** these are long-term decisions that affect the overall direction of the company. They are made by managers at the highest level.

**Tactical** these are medium-term decisions that are the stepping stones to achieving strategic decisions. They are made by middle level managers.

# Technologies outcomes

# 10

The following technologies outcomes relate to the Business area although they are more closely related to the subject area of Administration and IT.

It is not the purpose of this book to cover these outcomes and experiences in detail, however, we will provide some guidance below.

(There are lots of new business terms in this outcome. At the end of this chapter you will find a 'What this means' section to help you understand these new words.)

## Definition of outcome

**TCH 4–01c**

I can debate the possible future impact of new and emerging technologies on economic prosperity and the environment.

## Introduction to outcome

The scope of this outcome covers both individuals and businesses. In terms of business this could cover business practices, for example, how technology has changed the way the business operates, makes decisions and communicates with other people. **Entrepreneurs** have to come up with new ideas at all times.

## Development of outcome

### Transportation

New technology is changing the way people move and how goods are transported. Businesses are always being encouraged to be more environmentally friendly and managers have had to come up with new ideas. For example, new aircraft have features built into them that reduce carbon emissions and make them more environmentally friendly both in terms of pollution and the noise that they emit. Cars are now also being produced that run on environmentally friendly fuel or even electricity.

An electric car

## Mobile technology

The use of mobile or 'M' technology has allowed communication to take place while people are on the move and in different locations. This has enabled business to take place all over the world, instantly and at any time of day.

**Mobile technology** can be used for a number of things including:

- Sending a short message to other people via text (SMS).
- Taking and sending photographs to people.
- Accessing up-to-date news bulletins and business information.
- Sending and receiving email.
- Downloading and viewing reports from the Internet.

## Business information systems

Specialist computer programs and systems can be used in business for a number of different reasons.

**Information systems** are used to provide information to managers when monitoring the performance of a business and making decisions.

Expert systems can be used to provide specialist knowledge to people making decisions.

# Definition of outcome

**TCH 4–05a**

**By discussing the business, environmental, ethical and social implications of computer technology, I can begin to gain an understanding of the need for sustainability and accessibility.**

## Introduction to outcome

Computer technology in the modern world of business has many different uses. Businesses can make use of new technology to enable them to become more environmentally friendly, more ethical in their business practices and more socially responsible.

## Development of outcome

| Business aims | How technology could assist… |
|---|---|
| Become more environmentally friendly | ■ The use of alternative fuels in vehicles as well as more fuel-efficient vehicles.<br>■ Better logistics control to make best use of available resources for delivering goods.<br>■ The ability to monitor carbon emissions and take action to reduce them. |
| Have ethical business practices | ■ The use of ethical business practices – being fair in dealing with others in business. |
| Develop social awareness and responsibility | ■ Businesses that are socially aware are sensitive to people and other businesses that their business affects. They are responsible in the actions that they carry out in ensuring that they do not have a negative impact on others. Indeed, they may even carry out projects that involve the community in their work. |

# Definition of outcome

**TCH 4–06a/TCH 4–07a**

To facilitate the transfer of skills between the classroom and the world of work, I can select and use specialist equipment and appropriate software to develop administrative and management skills.

Whilst working in a simulated or real workplace, I can select and use appropriate software to carry out a range of tasks which support business and entrepreneurial activities.

## Introduction to outcome

These outcomes look at how equipment and software can be used in business for a range of administrative and management activities. You may have used some of these pieces of equipment/software already or have seen them in school or at home. Your teacher may show you how some of these work. The activities throughout this book could be completed using specialist software including word processing and presentation software.

## Development of outcome

### Equipment

A range of equipment can be used in the office to assist in the day-to-day running of the business.

A **photocopier** is used to make multiple copies of documents. It can copy documents as many times as required and can print double-sided, staple and reduce or enlarge the size of the document being copied.

A **scanner** is used to make a paper copy of a document available electronically. This could then be stored on a computer, network, uploaded to the Internet or emailed to those who require it.

A **fax machine** is used to send a hard copy of a document to another person. The person receiving the document receives an exact copy of what the document looks like.

A **multi-function device** (MFD) combines the functions of a photocopier, scanner and fax machine. It is becoming very popular in the modern office because of the range of functions and tasks it can carry out.

A **PDA** is commonly used to help a person organise their day and the range of tasks they have to carry out. It is a handheld device that can be carried around and accessed at any time.

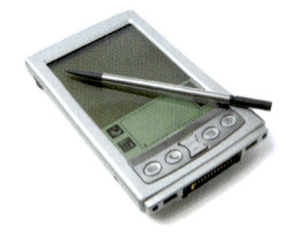

A **notebook** or **laptop** is a small computer that is portable and can be carried around easily by the user. It can perform all of the tasks that a normal desktop computer can perform.

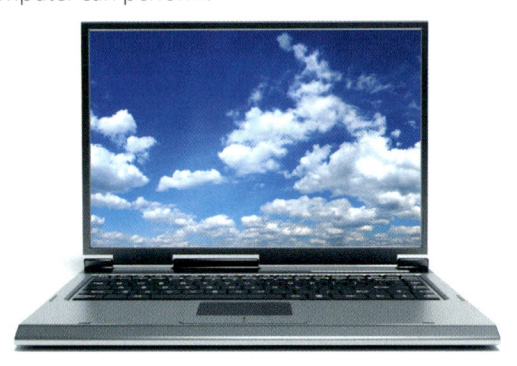

## Software

Software is installed onto a computer system to enable the user to perform a variety of tasks. Each piece of software is designed to carry out a specific range of tasks. Common pieces of software found in the office are described below.

**Word processing** software is used to present text and to communicate written information. It could be used to type out a letter to a customer or a memorandum to a colleague.

**Spreadsheet** software is used to store, edit and arrange numbers. Financial information, such as sales figures, can be recorded and analysed by managers. Formulae can be inserted into the spreadsheet to provide a range of information to managers when making decisions. Charts and graphs can also be created.

**Database** software is used to store information, for example, names and addresses of customers or suppliers. Queries can be performed to search for specific information, such as customers who live in a particular location. Reports can then be printed out with this information.

**Presentation** software is used to create electronic presentations. Your teacher may use presentation software to present some of your lessons! You could also use presentation software to deliver a talk in English, for example.

**Desktop publishing** can be used to create professional-looking posters, invitations, certificates and catalogues.

**Specialist accounting software** can be used to record the financial transactions of a business. Very detailed sales and purchase information can be recorded which is then used to create other financial documents. This software can also be used to prepare financial accounting statements and even calculate the wages for employees.

## The Internet

The Internet is a tool used by a large number of people. It has its uses not just at home but also for business. The Internet enables people and the entrepreneur to:

- research and find out information on competitors, new products and contact details for suppliers by typing in a URL (**uniform resource allocator**) so that a webpage is displayed
- send emails with information and attachments to other people no matter where they are in the world
- upload and share files and folders so that people can access information from around the world at any time.

The Internet is a great resource in that people can access it at any time. Business does not stop and the Internet enables people to communicate regardless of the country or time zone that they are in.

## Definition of outcome

TCH 4–07b

**Whilst working in a simulated or real workplace, I can examine my work environment, considering office layout, ergonomic factors, and health and safety legislation.**

## Introduction to outcome

Modern businesses must follow legislation which is designed to protect its employees. Some of this relates to the environment in which employees work. For example, all employees are entitled to work in a safe office environment with the correct equipment provided for them to carry out their work. This could include having the correct desk and chair. **Ergonomics** refers to the design of equipment and how it interacts with the user.

## Development of outcome

Office layout is important and may be dictated by the type of business. It contributes to effective working practices. Some businesses have **open-plan** layouts where all employees work in one large space. Other businesses have a **cellular** layout where the space is divided up into separate offices.

An open-plan office

A cellular office

Health and safety is a responsibility of everyone – employers and employees. This is laid out by the law. Employers have a responsibility to provide necessary training and equipment for people to do their jobs safely. Employees have a responsibility to look after themselves and other people, and any equipment they use. This is why it is important, for example, that you do not drink while you are in a computer room, in order to protect the computers from damage and yourself and anyone else from electrocution. Employees should comply with any instruction given by their employer and report any health and safety issues immediately.

## Revision tasks

1. Describe what is meant by 'M' technology.
2. Give three examples of when M technology could be used in business.
3. Describe what is meant by an 'expert system'.
4. Give two examples of what a business could do to achieve its aim of becoming more environmentally friendly.
5. Describe what a photocopier is.
6. Identify what the initials MFD stand for.
7. Describe what an MFD is.
8. Identify what the initials PDA stand for.
9. Describe what a PDA is.
10. Give an example of a task that could be carried out by a word processor.
11. Give an example of a task that could be carried out by a spreadsheet.
12. Give an example of a task that could be carried out by a database.
13. Describe what is meant by a database query.
14. Describe the purpose of accounting software.
15. Identify what the initials URL stand for.
16. Describe what a URL is.
17. Describe the features of an open-plan office layout.
18. Describe the features of a cellular office layout.
19. Identify one responsibility of an employer with regard to health and safety.
20. Identify one responsibility of an employee with regard to health and safety.
21. Describe the term 'ergonomics'.
22. Give a reason why ergonomics is important.

## What this means

**Accessibility** how easy it is to use something.

**Cellular** office layout where the space is divided up into individual spaces/offices.

**Entrepreneur** the person who comes up with a business idea and combines the four factors of production (land, labour, capital and enterprise) to make it a success.

**Ergonomics** ergonomics refers to the design of equipment and how it interacts with the user.

**Ethical** behaving ethically means acting in a responsible and sensible way.

**Fax machine** a piece of equipment used to send a hard copy document to another person.

**Information systems** specialist computer programs used to carry out specialist tasks.

**Mobile technology** using mobile phones to communicate with other people and to perform a variety of tasks (e.g. to access the Internet).

**Multi-function device (MFD)** a piece of equipment which combines the functions of a photocopier, scanner and fax machine.

**Notebook/laptop** a small portable computer.

**Open plan** office layout where all employees work in one large open space.

**PDA** a handheld organising device.

**Photocopier** a piece of equipment used to make lots of copies of a document.

**Scanner** a piece of equipment used to make an electronic copy of something.

**Software** instructions on how a computer should operate a program.

**Sustainability** this is usually referred to in the context of how using something now will impact on the ability to use it again in the future.

**Uniform resource locator (URL)** the address typed into a browser to access the Internet. It usually begins with 'http://www'.

# Part 2

## Value Added Tasks (VATs)

# VAT 1

## Introduction to the task

This task is group based. You should work in groups of two or three to come up with a business idea, research it and present it to the class.

### Aims
- Develop research skills
- Develop team working skills
- Improve written communication skills
- Improve presenting skills
- Organise information
- Opportunity for peer assessment to take place
- Develop skills in entrepreneurship
- Become an effective contributor
- Develop ICT skills

### Knowledge & Skills
- Types of business organisations
- Business objectives
- Entrepreneurship
- Sources of finance
- Presentation skills
- ICT skills
- Teamwork

### Link to CfE outcomes
- SOC 4-20b
- SOC 4-21a
- SOC 4-21b
- TCH 4-06a
- LIT 4-02a
- LIT 4-03a
- LIT 4-06a
- LIT 4-09a
- LIT 4-10a
- LIT 4-15a
- LIT 4-21a
- LIT 4-24a

### Preparation/resources
- Access to ICT and the Internet
- Business Plan template
- Peer assessment sheet (see p.92)
- Self-assessment sheet (see p.93)

## Description of the task

1. Arrange yourselves in groups of two or three.
2. Appoint a managing director who has responsibility for ensuring the task is completed on time.
3. Prepare a summary of your business idea.
4. Detail what your product or service is.
5. Detail why your product or service is important.
6. Create a name and logo for your business.
7. Identify who your customers will be.
8. Identify the type of business organisation.
9. Identify two advantages and two disadvantages of your chosen type of business.
10. State two business objectives for your organisation.
11. Identify two suitable sources of finance for starting your business.
12. Identify two advantages and two disadvantages of your chosen sources of finance.
13. You now need to gather your information and prepare to present it. You can choose the format of your business plan; it could be word processed or presented as a slide show. Whatever format you choose, make sure you write it very carefully and that it makes sense before you present it to your class.
14. Before presenting your business plan to your class, make sure you have decided who will say what. Remember, your class will be assessing your work!
15. Complete a self-assessment sheet for this task.
16. Complete a peer assessment sheet.

# VAT 2

## Introduction to the task

This is an individual task. You will work out your carbon footprint based on two different methods of travel to a destination chosen from a set list.

### Aims
- Develop research skills
- Improve written communication skills
- Organise information
- Develop problem-solving skills
- Independent learning
- Taking responsibility for own actions

### Knowledge & Skills
- ICT skills
- Environmental awareness
- Social responsibility
- Self-responsibility
- Decision making

### Link to CfE outcomes
- SOC 4–19a
- TCH 4–05a
- LIT 4–04a
- LIT 4–05a
- LIT 4–06a
- LIT 4–08a
- LIT 4–09a
- LIT 4–10a
- LIT 4–15a
- LIT 4–21a
- LIT 4–22a

### Preparation/resources
- Access to ICT and the Internet

## Description of the task

This task is about raising awareness of your social responsibility and the impact on the environment.

1. Plan your journey to one of the following cities:
   - London
   - Paris
   - Berlin.

2. Once you have chosen the city, you must find out how to travel there by air, train, bus and car.

3. Find out the distance to each of the cities travelling from your home town. You can use maps.google.co.uk to do this.

4. Identify the method of travel that you think will be the most environmentally friendly for travel to each city and give a reason for your choice in each case.

5. Use the website, www.carbonfootprint.com/calculator.aspx, to calculate the carbon footprint for each method of travel.

6. Write a short report of your findings for travel to each city. How did this compare to your initial thoughts on the most environmentally friendly method of travel to each city?

7. Suggest two other potential methods of travel that you could use to travel to the cities. These should be methods of travel that would result in a low carbon footprint.

8. Outline the impact that using these methods of travel could have on the following (these could be positive or negative):
   - The environment
   - Individuals
   - Business.

# VAT 3

## Introduction to the task

This is a group task. Appoint a leader for your team which should have three or four members. Your task will involve researching an environmental recycling activity. You will produce a written report and also present your findings to your class.

### Aims
- Develop research skills
- Develop teamworking skills
- Improve written communication skills
- Improve presenting skills
- Organise information
- Opportunity for peer assessment to take place
- Become an effective contributor

### Knowledge & Skills
- ICT skills
- Environmental awareness
- Social responsibility
- Self-responsibility
- Decision making
- Teamwork

### Link to CfE outcomes
- SOC 4–19a
- TCH 4–05a
- LIT 4–04a
- LIT 4–05a
- LIT 4–06a
- LIT 4–08a
- LIT 4–09a
- LIT 4–10a
- LIT 4–15a
- LIT 4–21a
- LIT 4–22a

### Preparation/resources
- Access to ICT and the Internet
- Peer assessment sheet (see p.92)
- Self-assessment sheet (see p.93)

## Description of the task

1. Arrange yourselves in groups of three or four.
2. Appoint a team leader who has responsibility for ensuring the task is completed on time.
3. Research the level and type of environmental recycling that takes place in the department in your school and in the school in general.
4. Investigate whether or not there are environmental and recycling policies in place and if they are being followed.
5. Evaluate the effectiveness of the policies.
6. Make suggestions as to how the environmental and recycling record of the school departments and the school can be improved. How could this be encouraged across the school?
7. Produce a report to summarise all your findings.
8. Produce a short presentation using PowerPoint software to present your findings to the class. There should be a maximum of 10 slides.
9. Make a poster to encourage people working and learning in your school to recycle.
10. Complete a self-assessment sheet for this task.
11. Complete a peer assessment sheet.

# VAT 4

## Introduction to the task

This task involves you analysing and presenting the results of a survey in the use of new technologies. You will need to calculate percentages, the average, mode and median as well as having to prepare various charts.

### Aims
- Develop numeracy skills
- Develop information gathering and handling skills
- Use ICT to prepare graphical information
- Develop oral and written communication skills
- Develop problem-solving and reasoning skills

### Knowledge & Skills
- Technology: mobile phones, PDAs and laptops
- Analysing the results of a survey
- Presenting the results of a survey in graphical and numerical form

### Link to CfE outcomes
- MNU 3–07a
- MNU 4–07a
- MNU 4–20a
- SOC 4–20c
- TCH 4–01c
- TCH 4–06a
- LIT 4–21a
- LIT 4–22a

### Preparation/resources
- Access to ICT and spreadsheet software
- Access to a calculator

## Description of the task

You are the Sales Manager for a company called Techno Whizz, a company that specialises in being at the forefront of new technology, mobile phones and computers. They recently carried out a survey of 200 customers and the results of this survey are given below.

Your task is to look at the results of the survey and then answer the questions which follow.

| Number of people questioned | 200 |
| Number of people with a mobile phone | 178 |
| Number of people with a PDA | 89 |
| Number of people with a laptop | 156 |

From the 178 people with a mobile phone, the number of people with specific types of mobile phones are:

| Most recent iPhone | 78 |
| Most recent Blackberry | 35 |
| Most recent Nokia | 24 |
| Most recent Sony Ericson | 23 |

Mobile phone users were also asked to say which age group they belonged to. The results are on the following page:

| Age 16 | 2 | Age 26 | 2 | Age 36 | 10 | Age 46 | 0 | Age 56 | 4 |
|---|---|---|---|---|---|---|---|---|---|
| Age 17 | 0 | Age 27 | 1 | Age 37 | 2 | Age 47 | 6 | Age 57 | 8 |
| Age 18 | 4 | Age 28 | 3 | Age 38 | 3 | Age 48 | 4 | Age 58 | 2 |
| Age 19 | 0 | Age 29 | 2 | Age 39 | 0 | Age 49 | 7 | Age 59 | 1 |
| Age 20 | 5 | Age 30 | 3 | Age 40 | 9 | Age 50 | 8 | Age 60 | 2 |
| Age 21 | 4 | Age 31 | 4 | Age 41 | 3 | Age 51 | 1 | Age 61 | 4 |
| Age 22 | 5 | Age 32 | 9 | Age 42 | 0 | Age 52 | 4 | Age 62 | 3 |
| Age 23 | 0 | Age 33 | 12 | Age 43 | 4 | Age 53 | 3 | Age 63 | 0 |
| Age 24 | 0 | Age 34 | 11 | Age 44 | 0 | Age 54 | 6 | Age 64 | 1 |
| Age 25 | 6 | Age 35 | 10 | Age 45 | 0 | Age 55 | 0 | Age 65 | 0 |

From the 89 people with a PDA, 56 people said that they use it for work purposes.

From the 156 people with a laptop, the main reason for having one was:

| For work use only | 23 |
|---|---|
| For personal use only | 34 |
| For work and personal use | 86 |

## Questions

1. Write a down a brief description of a mobile phone, PDA and laptop.
2. Give a reason why each piece of equipment could be used by a teleworker and/or homeworker.
3. Calculate the percentage of people with a mobile phone, PDA and laptop.
4. Present the results of the above as a clearly labelled bar chart.
5. Calculate the number of people who did not say which type of mobile phone they owned.
6. Using the answer from question 5, together with the information given, prepare a pie chart which shows the proportion of people who own each different type of mobile phone. Include percentages on your chart.
7. Using your chart to help, recommend which type of mobile phone your company should sell and recommend reasons why.
8. Calculate the average age of the mobile phone user.
9. What is the mode of the mobile phone age user?
10. What is the median of the mobile phone age user?
11. What age group would you recommend that your company focuses its sales and marketing promotions to? Why?
12. What percentage of people use a PDA for work purposes?
13. Calculate the number of people who did not say why they used a laptop computer.
14. Using the answer from question 13, together with the information given, prepare a pie chart which shows the proportion of people who use a laptop for different reasons. Include the actual number of people on your chart (not percentages).
15. Give two disadvantages of specialising in selling new technology.

# VAT 5

## Introduction to the task

This task requires you to create an organisation chart and to answer various questions about it. It covers internal organisation and decision making.

### Aims
- Develop research skills
- Gather and present information

### Knowledge & Skills
- Decision making
- Organisation and management skills
- Internal and external factors

### Link to CfE outcomes
- SOC 4–20b
- SOC 4–22a
- SOC 4–22b
- LIT 4–06a
- LIT 4–21a
- LIT 4–22a

### Preparation/resources
- Paper
- Coloured pens
- Ruler

## Description of the task

1. Draw up an organisation chart of your school and then answer the following questions. The chart should be prepared neatly. Note: The organisation chart must cover all levels.
2. Who has the most responsibility in the school?
3. How many layers are there in the school?
4. Is this a hierarchical (pyramid) or a flat structure?
5. Give an advantage of the structure identified in question 4.
6. Give a disadvantage of the structure identified in question 4.
7. How many departments are there in the school?
8. Name the strategic managers in the school.
9. Name the tactical managers in the school.
10. Name the operational managers in the school.
11. Which type of manager has the most responsibility and authority?
12. Which type of manager has the least responsibility and authority?
13. Give an example of when technology is used in your school.
14. Give an example of a piece of legislation that your school must follow.
15. What impact does this piece of legislation have on your school?
16. Give an example of something that your school has done to become more environmentally friendly
17. Identify the sector of business that a school belongs to.
18. Identify the main aim of your school.
19. Identify three stakeholders of your school.
20. Describe the interests of the three stakeholders of your school that you have identified in question 19.
21. Describe the influence that the local council has on your school.

# VAT 6

## Introduction to the task

This task is group based. It deals with basic economics using a familiar context. You are required to work in groups of three or four. Appoint a team leader who will report back to the rest of the class. You are required to use the Internet to research an advertisement for a product with which you are familiar.

### Aims

- Develop research skills
- Gather and present information
- Develop teamworking skills
- Improve written communication skills
- Improve presenting skills
- Organise information
- Opportunity for peer assessment to take place
- Become an effective contributor

### Knowledge & Skills

- Decision making
- Teamwork
- ICT skills development

### Link to CfE outcomes

- SOC 4–20a
- LIT 4–06a
- LIT 4–21a
- LIT 4–22a

### Preparation/resources

- Access to the Internet
- Word processing software
- Presentation software
- Peer assessment sheet (see p.92)
- Self-assessment sheet (see p.93)

## Description of the task

1. Arrange yourselves in groups of three or four.
2. Appoint a team leader who has responsibility for ensuring the task is completed on time.
3. Use the Internet to research advertisements for products that you use or are interested in buying.
4. Identify one advert that is effective in selling one of your chosen products to the consumer.
5. List your reasons for the advert being effective.
6. Is the product that you have chosen a need or a want?
7. Identify one advert that is not effective in selling one of your chosen products to the consumer.
8. List reasons for the advert not being effective.
9. Suggest ways to improve the advert that would make the product more attractive to consumers.
10. Is the product that you have chosen a need or a want?
11. Prepare a short report of your findings.
12. Create a short presentation to support your report (maximum of 10 slides).
13. Complete a self-assessment sheet for this task.
14. Complete a peer assessment sheet.

# VAT 7

## Introduction to the task

You can do this task in groups or as an individual. It encourages exploration of layout and ergonomics.

### Aims
- Develop research skills
- Gather and present information
- Develop team working skills
- Improve written communication skills
- Improve presenting skills
- Organise information
- Opportunity for peer assessment to take place
- Become an effective contributor

### Knowledge & Skills
- Decision making
- Teamwork
- ICT skills development
- Ergonomics
- Office layout

### Link to CfE outcomes
- TCH 4–07b
- LIT 4–06a
- LIT 4–21a
- LIT 4–22a

### Preparation/resources
- Access to the Internet
- Word processing software
- Presentation software
- Workstation assessment sheet
- Peer assessment sheet (if appropriate) (see p.92)
- Self-assessment sheet (if appropriate) (see p.93)

## Description of the task

1. Arrange yourselves in groups of three or four, or work individually as instructed by your teacher.
2. If appropriate, appoint a team leader who has responsibility for ensuring the task is completed on time.
3. Look at the layout of your classroom.
4. Make a plan of your classroom layout on a piece of paper.
5. Why is the classroom laid out this way?
6. Does the classroom layout make good use of the space?
7. Does the classroom layout help with your teaching and learning?
8. What could be done to improve the layout of your classroom? Devise a new plan on a piece of paper and write down the reasons for making changes.
9. Carry out a workstation assessment on one of your friends using the workstation assessment sheet (p.84).
10. Carry out a health and safety check of your classroom by making a note of any potential hazards.
11. Prepare a short report of your findings about classroom layout, health and safety and the workstations in the classroom.
12. Create a short presentation to support your report (maximum of 10 slides).
13. Complete a peer assessment sheet if you worked in a group.
14. Complete a self-assessment sheet if you worked on your own.
15. Create a simple health and safety poster for your classroom outlining five key rules that will make your classroom a safe place to work.

# Workstation Assessment Sheet

Name:                                                    Date of assessment:

| Equipment display screen assessment | Yes ✔ | No ✔ |
|---|---|---|
| Is the display screen image clear? | | |
| Are the characters readable? | | |
| Is the image free of flicker and movement? | | |
| Is the brightness and/or contrast adjustable? | | |
| Does the screen swivel and tilt? | | |
| Is the screen free of glare and reflection? | | |

| Equipment keyboard assessment | Yes ✔ | No ✔ |
|---|---|---|
| Can you tilt the keyboard? | | |
| Is there enough space to rest hands in front of the keyboard? | | |
| Is the keyboard comfortable to use? | | |
| Can you find a comfortable keying position? | | |
| Is the keyboard glare free? | | |
| Are the characters on the keys easily readable? | | |

| Equipment work desk assessment | Yes ✔ | No ✔ |
|---|---|---|
| Does the furniture fit the work and the user? | | |
| Is the work surface large enough for documents, keyboard etc.? | | |
| Is there adequate space for you to adopt a comfortable position? | | |
| Is the surface free of glare reflections? | | |
| Is there a document holder provided? | | |

| Equipment work chair assessment | Yes ✔ | No ✔ |
|---|---|---|
| Is the chair stable and has easy freedom of movement? | | |
| Is it possible to adjust the backrest (height and tilt), the chair height and the seat tilt? | | |
| Is your chair comfortable? | | |
| Is a footrest required? | | |

| Environment space assessment | Yes ✔ | No ✔ |
|---|---|---|
| Is there enough room to change positions and vary movement? | | |
| Are there any obstructions nearby? | | |

| Environment assessment | Yes ✔ | No ✔ |
|---|---|---|
| Are the levels of light, noise and heat comfortable? | | |
| Is there appropriate adjustable lighting? | | |
| Are the light fittings free from glare? | | |
| Does heat given off from workstation equipment cause the user any discomfort? | | |
| Does any noise pollution from the display screen distract or discomfort the user? | | |

# VAT 8

## Introduction to the task

This task introduces pupils to preparing budgets.

### Aims
- Develop numeracy skills
- Develop information gathering and handling skills
- Use spreadsheet software to prepare budgets

### Knowledge & Skills
- Cash budgets
- Money management
- Spreadsheet skills

### Link to CfE outcomes
- SOC 4–21b
- TCH 4–06a
- LIT 4–21a
- LIT 4–22a
- MNU 3–09b

### Preparation/resources
- Calculator
- Spreadsheet software

## Description of the task

1. Using the information given below, complete the budget for Puplee Pet Products Ltd for March and April.

   The Opening Balance for March was £5000.

   Sales for March was £5000 and April £5500

   Payments for March were: Wages £50, Advertising £100, Rent £230 and Heating £150.

   Payments for April were: Wages £100, Advertising £140, Rent £230 and Heating £250.

2. What month had the highest total payments?

3. What month had the best closing balance?

4. Using your spreadsheet skills, prepare the budget on the following page. You should insert **formulae** to calculate the opening balance, total cash, total payments and closing balance.

5. Using your spreadsheet skills, prepare a bar chart showing payments for March. Make sure you label your chart appropriately.

| Budget of Puplee Pet Products Ltd for March and April | | |
|---|---|---|
| | March | April |
| Opening balance | | |
| **Receipts** | | |
| Sales | | |
| Total cash | | |
| **Payments** | | |
| Wages | | |
| Advertising | | |
| Rent | | |
| Heating | | |
| Total payments | | |
| Closing balance | | |

# VAT 9

## Introduction to the task

You will record your experiences in using ICT in real life contexts for different purposes.

### Aims
- Develop ICT skills in a range of contexts

### Knowledge & Skills
- Word processing
- Spreadsheets
- Databases
- Presentation skills
- Email

### Link to CfE outcomes
- TCH 4–06a
- TCH 4–07a
- LIT 4–21a
- LIT 4–22a

### Preparation/resources
- Access to appropriate software

## Description of the task

Use the sheet on the following page to record when you have used different software packages in everyday situations. For example, if you have used a word-processing package in English to write an essay, you can write down that you have done this. Or you might use a spreadsheet to analyse numbers and create graphs in Maths. If you find that you don't use a particular package then your teacher will give you a task to do to show that you can use it.

You are required to record any problems that you came across when using ICT and to write down what you did to solve them.

To show that you have achieved these outcomes, you should use each software package at least twice. An example has been completed for you.

### Example

| Software package: Word processing | Date used: 1 November |
|---|---|
| What I used the package for:<br><br>I used a word-processing package to create a menu in Home Economics. | Different skills/functions I used:<br><br>- I had to create and save a new document. I changed the font and its size.<br>- I added in two graphics and I centred some of the text.<br>- I put my name and class into the footer.<br>- I printed the document after I had checked it for any errors. |

# Software package comparison sheet

| Software package: Word processing Task 1 | Date used: |
|---|---|
| What I used the package for: | Different skills/functions I used: |

| Software package: Word processing Task 2 | Date used: |
|---|---|
| What I used the package for: | Different skills/functions I used: |

| Software package: Spreadsheet Task 1 | Date used: |
|---|---|
| What I used the package for: | Different skills/functions I used: |

| Software package: Spreadsheet Task 2 | Date used: |
|---|---|
| What I used the package for: | Different skills/functions I used: |

| Software package: Database Task 1 | Date used: |
|---|---|
| What I used the package for: | Different skills/functions I used: |

| Software package: Database Task 1 | Date used: |
|---|---|
| What I used the package for: | Different skills/functions I used: |

# Software package comparison sheet cont...

| Software package: Presentation Task 1 | Date used: |
|---|---|
| What I used the package for: | Different skills/functions I used: |

| Software package: Presentation Task 2 | Date used: |
|---|---|
| What I used the package for: | Different skills/functions I used: |

| Software package: Email Task 1 | Date used: |
|---|---|
| What I used the package for: | Different skills/functions I used: |

| Software package: Email Task 2 | Date used: |
|---|---|
| What I used the package for: | Different skills/functions I used: |

| Problems | Solutions |
|---|---|
| 1 | |
| 2 | |
| 3 | |

# Appendices

Photocopiable sheets

VATs mapping grid

# Peer Assessment Sheet

Name of group:

| Checklist questions | Yes | No |
| --- | --- | --- |
| Did everyone in the group participate? | | |
| Did the group finish their task on time? | | |
| Did the group follow all instructions? | | |
| Did the group ask for help when they got stuck? | | |
| Did everyone in the group come up with ideas? | | |
| Does my teacher think our group worked well? | | |

**Two stars and a wish**

**Two things we did well:**

1

2

**One thing we need to improve on next time:**

1

Overall, the group would rate their performance as (tick or circle):

**Gold**       **Silver**       **Bronze**

# Self-assessment Sheet

Name:

| Checklist questions | Yes | No |
|---|---|---|
| Did I participate in the task? | | |
| Did I complete everything that was asked of me to the best of my ability? | | |
| Did I complete everything on time? | | |
| Did I contribute ideas in group discussions? | | |
| Did I listen to the views of other people in group discussions? | | |
| Would the other people in my group think that I worked well? | | |

**Two stars and a wish**

Two things I did well:

1

2

One thing I need to improve on next time:

1

Overall, I would rate my performance as (tick or circle):

**Gold**   **Silver**   **Bronze**

© Hodder Gibson 2011. Copying permitted within the purchasing institution only.

APPENDIX  VATs mapping grid

# Value Added Tasks (VATs) mapping grids

## Links to Social Studies and Technologies outcomes

| | SOC 4-19a | SOC 4-20a | SOC 4-20b | SOC 4-20c | SOC 4-21a | SOC 4-21b | SOC 4-22a | SOC 4-22b | TCH 4-01c | TCH 4-05a | TCH 4-06a | TCH 4-07a | TCH 4-07b |
|---|---|---|---|---|---|---|---|---|---|---|---|---|---|
| Task 1 | | | | | | | | | | | ✓ | | |
| Task 2 | ✓ | | | | | | | | | ✓ | | | |
| Task 3 | ✓ | | | | | | | | | ✓ | | | |
| Task 4 | | | | | | | | | ✓ | | | | |
| Task 5 | | | ✓ | | | | ✓ | | | | ✓ | | |
| Task 6 | | ✓ | | | | | | ✓ | | | | | |
| Task 7 | | | | ✓ | ✓ | | | | | | | | ✓ |
| Task 8 | | | | | | ✓ | | | | | ✓ | | |
| Task 9 | | | | | | | | | | | ✓ | ✓ | |

## Links to Literacy and Numeracy outcomes

| | LIT 4-02a | LIT 4-03a | LIT 4-04a | LIT 4-05a | LIT 4-06a | LIT 4-08a | LIT 4-09a | LIT 4-10a | LIT 4-15a | LIT 4-21a | LIT 4-22a | LIT 4-24a | MNU 3-07b | MNU 3-09b | MNU 4-07b | MNU 4-20b |
|---|---|---|---|---|---|---|---|---|---|---|---|---|---|---|---|---|
| Task 1 | ✓ | ✓ | | | ✓ | | ✓ | ✓ | ✓ | ✓ | ✓ | | | | | |
| Task 2 | | | ✓ | ✓ | ✓ | ✓ | ✓ | ✓ | ✓ | ✓ | ✓ | | | | | |
| Task 3 | | | ✓ | ✓ | ✓ | ✓ | ✓ | ✓ | ✓ | ✓ | ✓ | | | | | |
| Task 4 | | | | | | | | | | ✓ | ✓ | ✓ | ✓ | | | |
| Task 5 | | | | | ✓ | | | | | ✓ | ✓ | | | | | |
| Task 6 | | | | | ✓ | | | | | ✓ | ✓ | | | | | |
| Task 7 | | | | | ✓ | | | | | ✓ | ✓ | | | | | |
| Task 8 | | | | | | | | | | ✓ | ✓ | | | ✓ | | |
| Task 9 | | | | | | | | | | ✓ | ✓ | | | | ✓ | ✓ |

# Index

accessibility 72
accounting software 69
administration/IT departments 51, 54
attitudes 2

bank statements 44
banks 43–4
basic economic problem 14–15
BP (British Petroleum) 12–13
budgets 45–6, 55
bus transport company 3–5
business failure 15–17
Business Gateway 40
business information systems 65
business objectives 25–8
business organisations 20–3, 50–7

capital 31, 39
cellular office layout 70, 72
central government 28
charities 23, 24, 28
communication 56, 65
competition
    and business failure 15, 16
    and decision making 62
computer technology 66–9
contracts of employment 34, 36
corporate social responsibility 5
corporation tax 40
credit cards 46–7
cultures 2

databases 69
debentures 39
debit cards 46–7
decision making 56, 58–63
delayering 57
demand 14, 15, 16
departments 51–5
desktop publishing 69
dividends 31

economic factors
    and business failure 15–18
    and decision making 61
economics 14–15

economies of scale 16
Enterprise Finance Guarantee 40
entrepreneurs 64, 72
environmental factors, and decision making 61
environmental issues
    Greenpeace and BP 11–13
    transportation 64
ergonomics 70, 72
ethical behaviour 72
European Union funds 39
expert systems 65
external factors, and decision making 60–2, 63
external sources of finance 38

fax machines 68, 72
finance
    and decision making 59
    sources 37–40
finance departments 51, 53
FirstGroup plc 3–5
fixed-term employment 33, 34, 36
flat structure 56–7
flexitime 33, 36
four 'Ps' (price, product, place, promotion) 54–5
franchises 3, 23, 24
full time working 33, 36
functional departments 51–5

government assistance 39–40
grants 39
Greenpeace 11

health and safety issues 70
hierarchical structure 56
hire purchase 38
homeworking 33, 36
human resources (HR) departments 51, 52

industrial action 31
influence 26, 27, 28
information, and decision making 59
information systems 65, 72
interest 26, 27, 28
internal factors, and decision making 59–60, 63
internal sources of finance 38
the Internet 69

internet banking 44

job-shares 33, 36

laptops 68, 72
lending 47
limited companies 22, 24, 27, 31
local government 28
long-term loans 39
long-term sources of finance 39

M technology 65
management
    and business failure 15
    and decision making 60
marketing departments 51, 54–5
MFDs (multi-function devices) 68, 72
mobile technology 65, 72
mortgages 39
multi-function devices (MFDs) 68, 72

notebooks 68, 72

objectives, of business 25–8
office layouts 70
open-plan cellular office layout 70, 72
operational decisions 59, 63
operations departments 51, 53
organisation chart 51
organisational structure 56–7
organisations 2, 20–3, 50–7
overdrafts 38

part time working 33, 36
partnerships 22, 24, 27, 31
PDAs (personal digital assistants) 36, 68
permanent employment 33, 34, 36
personal digital assistants (PDAs) 36, 68
photocopiers 67, 72
political factors, and decision making 60
presentation software 69
price, product, place, promotion (four 'Ps') 54–5
Prince's Trust 40
private limited companies 24, 50–7
private sector organisations 26, 27, 31
procedures 56
public corporations 28
public limited companies 22, 24
public sector organisations 23, 26, 28
public transport companies 3–8

rail transport company 3–5
recession 14, 15, 17
research and development departments 51, 55
responsibility 56
responsible lending policies 47
restructure 6
Ryanair 6–8

salary 31
scanners 67, 72
shareholders 22, 27
shares 31
short-term loans 38
short term sources of finance 38
social factors, and decision making 61
software 68–9, 72
sole traders 21, 24, 27, 31
specialist accounting software 69
spreadsheets 69
stakeholders 26–8, 31
Stock Exchange 6
strategic decisions 59, 63
supply 16, 17
sustainability 72

tactical decisions 59, 63
taxes 16, 40
technological factors, and decision making 61
technology
    and business information systems 65
    and communication 65
    and decision making 60
    and transportation 64
teleworking 33, 36
temporary employment 33, 34, 36
trade credit 38
transportation 64 *see also* Ryanair

unemployment 16, 17
UNITE union 4
URLs (uniform resource allocator) 70, 72

voluntary sector organisations 23, 24, 26, 28, 31
voluntary sports clubs 28

word processing 68
work environments 70
working practices 32–5